Free movement and beyond

Agenda setting for Brexit Britain

Edited by Kate Hudson

publicreading
ROOMS
www.prruk.org

Published in 2017 by Public Reading Rooms
Visit our website at www.prruk.org
© with each author
All rights reserved
ISBN 9780995535220

Contents

Foreword: The attack on freedom of movement is an attack on us all

DIANE ABBOTT MP

Last year's Tory party conference represented a sharp rightwards turn. The rhetorical focus for all their attacks was foreigners, in work, in schools, in our health service. The political strategy was formed by the realisation that we cannot be in the Single Market and opt out of freedom of movement. So they have opted for anti-immigration and impoverishment, getting out of the Single Market in order to pursue a reactionary agenda on immigration.

When Jeremy Hunt announced his anti-foreigner plan for the UK to become 'self-sufficient' in doctors, he also included a reactionary new measure to be imposed on UK-trained doctors. But this was only one of the barrage of assaults on overseas workers announced at the conference.

The Tories were forced to retreat on their plan that companies are to be named and shamed for employing overseas workers. Yet students and scientists will still be turned away. The whole conference was an exercise in scapegoating. The crisis is caused by Tory policy and their allies and supporters, exploitative employers, rapacious landlords, rip-off private owners of formerly nationalised industries. It is not caused by immigrants.

Now under the Hunt plan, doctors trained in this country will have to work in the NHS for four years. Otherwise, they will have to repay the cost of their training, which the British Medical Association estimates at over a quarter of a million pounds minimum.

This demonstrates a general law that the labour movement has understood for a long time: an injury to one is an injury to all. Attacks on overseas workers always rebound and include regressive measures against domestic workers too. So, in a futile effort to restrict overseas workers the Tories are also ordering restrictions on workers trained here too, curbing their freedom of movement.

For the NHS, the drive towards a foreigner-free doctor workforce would be a disaster. There are 100,000 overseas doctors in the UK. There is already a significant shortage of doctors. Of course we should be training more doctors and other health professionals in this country, just as we should be training all sorts of skilled and highly-skilled workers across a range of sectors. But the idea that that we could or should seek to eliminate overseas doctors from the NHS and become 'self-sufficient' is a reactionary fantasy.

Even if all of Hunt's additional new 1,500 UK-trained doctors don't drop out, and even if he successfully compels them all to work for four years, this would not close the doctor shortage. It will grow and the number of overseas doctors will rise under current plans. Otherwise the NHS will go into absolute crisis.

It is a scandal that Theresa May and Liam Fox want to use EU workers here as a 'bargaining chip' in negotiations with EU countries. They should be offered guarantees of work and residency. But these existing workers here will also need replacing, and we cannot force UK-trained doctors to work here indefinitely. We need freedom of movement for doctors and other health professionals simply for the continued existence of the NHS.

WORKERS' RIGHTS

The demagogic campaign against foreigners that was first championed by UKIP and is now mainstream Tory policy obscures a key point. It is important to remember that freedom of movement is a workers' right.

In all societies where there are significantly greater freedoms for business and for capital than for workers, then in practice workers' rights are severely curtailed. Business is at a huge advantage. This reaches an extreme in the most authoritarian countries.

So for example, the 'pass laws' in apartheid South Africa made black workers non-residents without rights in their own country, while they suffered the most brutal exploitation in the mines and elsewhere. Even in this country, the Poor Laws formerly restricted the movement of workers from one parish to another. They could not seek poor relief outside their own parish if they were unemployed and went looking for work. The Poor Laws were only effectively abolished by the Labour Government in 1948.

In all these cases, business was able to freely establish wherever it chose. The effect is that workers' bargaining rights were severely curtailed, in some cases eliminated. They had to accept whatever jobs, and at whatever wages and terms that the employers in their locality chose. This is one of the key, overlooked issues in the current widespread assault on freedom of movement.

Economists for Brexit, the only grouping which produced economic arguments in favour of Leave, argued that UK manufacturing would be eliminated by the adoption of free trade and that inequality would widen dramatically as financial services would grow dramatically. This may be an exaggeration. More sober analysis from the UK Treasury is that in a European Economic Area agreement, government finances for services like the NHS will be £20 billion lower after 15 years, while falling back on World Trade Organisation rules reduces government finances by £45 billion. Public services would be decimated.

SCAPEGOATING

This Tory government is scapegoating foreigners to distract from its own complete failures of policy. Living standards are falling because of them, not migrants. The labour movement cannot accept living standards being lowered by Brexit and the attack on freedom of movement, and must stand to defend both.

The Tory government doesn't have an economic policy. Every time Theresa May gets up to speak the pound falls, and ordinary people literally pay higher prices as a result.

The Tories are desperate to shift the blame for this. They have declared open season on foreigners. That is why standing up to racism is so important. The broad forces of the labour movement, committed campaigners and the most oppressed sections of society can come together to combat all forms of xenophobia, anti-semitism and racism.

We can win. The Tory anti-foreigner policy would devastate our public services. It is already lowering living standards. It will lead to job losses. The majority will be worse off, and we have an alternative. Labour under Jeremy and John is committed to investment-led growth. This is the answer to the crisis, not a Tory campaign inspired by Enoch Powell.

Diane Abbott is MP for Hackney North and Stoke Newington and was appointed Shadow Home Secretary in October 2016.

Introduction

KATE HUDSON

As the referendum campaign on EU membership entered its final days, the tension and anger were palpable. Traditional fault lines in politics broke down as the divisions over Remain or Leave crossed and re-crossed through parties and movements where typically in a general election period sympathies would be predictable and tolerated.

The referendum came from pressure from the far right – driven by anti-immigration sentiment, fuelled by racism. As the campaign developed so the racism increased, insufficiently challenged and often fed, by the mainstream. The result was an open emergence of the extremist right. The last days of the campaign were overshadowed by the terrible killing of the Remain-supporting MP Jo Cox, her attacker shouting 'Britain First' – echoing the name of a far-right political party – as he fired into her face.

This disastrous turn of events tragically compounded the fact that this had been the most reactionary national campaign in British political history. A new low was achieved with a UKIP campaign advert, picturing queues of refugees under the heading: 'Breaking Point: Europe has failed us all – we must break free of the EU and take back our borders'. This was typical of much of the messaging and the narrative propagated by the Leave camp. If one could sum up the chief message of the Leave campaign it would be 'Blame immigrants for everything'. They peddled the politics of hate on baseless accusations and fictional figures. Those of us on the left who backed a 'critical Remain' position worked to convey the fact that if we don't have enough houses or jobs or services it's not because of migrants, it's because of government austerity policies that have failed to invest in our industry and economy.

The pro-Brexit left laid the country's economic problems at the door of the EU, arguing that Brexit would make socialism in Britain more likely, without the pro-austerity, anti-democratic EU. But the reality is these same policies – or worse – will be implemented by our government and we are already seeing that process unfolding as the prime minister pursues a hard Brexit. Indeed, it was Margaret Thatcher who brutally drove forward the neo-liberal cuts, deregulation, and anti-trade union agenda long before any other European country. The idea that Brexit would make a Corbyn-led Labour victory more likely – a view held by some on the left – was deeply misplaced. The Brexit referendum victory has strengthened the right in the Conservative party, drawing far-right support into its voter base, and making a Corbyn government less likely, not more likely. The impact of this on the everyday lives of immigrants within our communities has been savage. The anti-immigrant rhetoric, on which this swing to the right has turned, has built a hatred that has resulted in verbal and physical attacks, even killings.

An example of the mistaken thinking from left Brexit campaigners was the question of TTIP. Some argued that we should leave the EU to get out of free market agreements like TTIP. But as we leave the EU we'll face the same policies even if under a different name. All the mainstream Brexit arguments were premised on extreme free trade agreements and looser regulation – as bad as, or worse than, TTIP. At the moment it looks as though TTIP will be defeated by massive opposition from across Europe. Do we have the strength in Britain alone to overturn such a policy? We haven't managed to defeat our own government on cuts yet, or overturn its deregulation policies, or restore the trade union rights that Mrs Thatcher stripped us of in the 1980s.

Brexit will not be a loosening of the shackles of neo-liberalism, it will be an unmitigated compounding of the same policies by the British ruling class. In the left Remain view, we stand a better chance working together with the people of Europe, who are mounting their own massive political opposition to neo-liberalism. We have watched the advance of the left in some countries, where progressive policies have won popular support and have seen the struggles of European workers against the imposition of new labour laws, in defence of workers' rights, and to sustain or improve pay and conditions across Europe. We wish to be part of these shared struggles, working together across Europe – because the problems that we face stand more chance of a pro-people solution when we organise and act together.

Solidarity with these and other struggles is crucial – particularly those in defence of migrants and refugees, so often displaced through the wars and economic policies of our own and other so-called 'advanced' countries. But we also watch with grave concern the rise of the far right across Europe, in Hungary, Germany, The Netherlands, France and elsewhere. Many from the far right look to Brexit, calling for referenda in other countries, to deal a death blow to the EU. This is not a development from which left and progressive movements can benefit, particularly in the context of the Trump presidency in the USA. We need to consolidate our forces against this growing tendency and it is in all our interests to work together across Europe, not retreat into isolationism which will only assist and strengthen it.

This edited collection draws together the current thinking of many of Britain's most prominent 'critical Remainers' – those who argued to remain within the EU while seeking its democratic and progressive transformation. Working to contribute to the policy agenda for the Brexit process, the contributors address the controversial issue of free movement of people, defending it as central to Britain's economic success and as an advance for the working class across Europe. They debunk the myths that blame migration for economic woes and they condemn the racism that such myths give rise to. The contributors also outline policy proposals and principles in the areas of democracy, economics, trade policy, security policy, environmental legislation and workers' rights.

As the government triggers Article 50, the next stage of the struggle begins in earnest over the terms of the Brexit agreement. In truth we are fighting for our rights, our health, our education, our jobs, our homes and communities – and many will literally be fighting for their lives. The terms of the agreement will be highly contested and we 'critical Remainers' will work with others, in Britain and across Europe, to defend what has been won by the people over the generations, and we will fight to extend it. We refuse to go willingly into a hard Brexit and we will fight every step of the way, challenging the treaties, challenging the legislation – to help remake Britain as part of a refounded and democratic union of Europe. This book is a contribution to that process.

Why we must save the EU

YANIS VAROUFAKIS

The first German word I ever learned was Siemens. It was emblazoned on our sturdy 1950s fridge, our washing machine, the vacuum cleaner – on almost every appliance in my family's home in Athens. The reason for my parents' peculiar loyalty to the German brand was my uncle Panayiotis, who was Siemens' general manager in Greece from the mid-1950s to the late 1970s.

A Germanophile electrical engineer and a fluent speaker of Goethe's language, Panayiotis had convinced his younger sister – my mother – to take up the study of German; she even planned to spend a year in Hamburg to take up a Goethe Institute scholarship in the summer of 1967.

Alas, on 21 April 1967, my mother's plans were laid in ruins, along with our imperfect Greek democracy. For in the early hours of that morning, at the command of four army colonels, tanks rolled on to the streets of Athens and other major cities, and our country was soon enveloped in a thick cloud of neo-fascist gloom. It was also the day when Uncle Panayiotis's world fell apart.

Unlike my dad, who in the late 1940s had paid for his leftist politics with several years in concentration camps, Panayiotis was what today would be referred to as a neoliberal. Fiercely anti-communist, and suspicious of social democracy, he supported the American intervention in the Greek civil war in 1946 (on the side of my father's jailers). He backed the German Free Democratic party and the Greek Progressive party, which purveyed a blend of free-market economics with unconditional support for Greece's oppressive US-led state security machine.

His political views, and his position as the head of Siemens' operations in Greece, made Panayiotis a typical member of Greece's postwar ruling class. When state security forces or their stooges roughed up leftwing protesters, or even killed a brilliant member of parliament, Grigoris Lambrakis, in 1963, Panayiotis would grudgingly approve, convinced that these were unpleasant but necessary actions. My ears are still ringing with the rowdy exchanges he often had with Dad, over what he considered 'reasonable measures to defend democracy from its sworn enemies' – reasonable measures that my father had experienced first-hand, and from which he would never fully recover.

The heavy footprint of US agencies in Greek politics, even going so far as to engineer the dismissal of a popular centrist prime minister, Georgios Papandreou, in 1965, seemed to Panayiotis an acceptable trade-off: Greece had given up some sovereignty to western powers in exchange for freedom from a menacing eastern bloc lurking a short driving distance north of Athens. However, on that bleak April day in 1967, Panayiotis's life was turned upside down.

He simply could not tolerate that 'his' people (as he referred to the rightist army officers who had staged the coup and, more importantly, their American handlers) should dissolve parliament, suspend the constitution, and intern potential dissidents (including rightwing democrats) in football stadia, police stations and concentration camps. He had no great sympathy with the deposed centrist prime minister that the putschists and their US puppeteers were trying to keep out of government – but his worldview was torn asunder, leading him to a sudden spurt of almost comical radicalisation.

A few months after the military regime took power, Panayiotis joined an underground group called Democratic Defence, which consisted largely of other establishment liberals like himself – university professors, lawyers, and even a future prime minister. They planted a series of bombs around Athens, taking care to ensure there were no injuries, in order to demonstrate that the military regime was not in full control, despite its clampdown.

For a few years after the coup, Panayiotis appeared – even to his own mother – as yet another professional keeping his head down, minding his own business. No one had an inkling of his double life: corporate man during the day, subversive bomber by night. We were mostly relieved, meanwhile, that Dad had not disappeared again into some concentration camp.

My enduring memory of those years, in fact, is the crackling sound of a radio hidden under a red blanket in the middle of the living room in our Athens home. Every night at around nine, mum and dad would huddle together under the blanket – and upon hearing the muffled jingle announcing the beginning of the programme, followed by the voice of a German announcer, my own six-year-old imagination would travel from Athens to central Europe, a mythical place I had not visited yet except for the tantalising glimpses offered by an illustrated Brothers Grimm book I had in my bedroom.

Deutsche Welle, the German international radio station that my parents were listening to, became their most precious ally against the crushing power of state propaganda at home: a window looking out to faraway democratic Europe. At the end of each of its hour-long special broadcasts on Greece, my parents and I would sit around the dining table while they mulled over the latest news.

I didn't fully understand what they were discussing, but this neither bored nor upset me. For I was gripped by a sense of excitement at the strangeness of our predicament: that, to find out what was happening in our very own Athens, we had to travel, through the airwaves, and veiled by a red blanket, to a place called Germany.

The reason for the red blanket was a grumpy old neighbour called Gregoris. Gregoris was known for his connections with the secret police and his penchant for spying on my parents; in particular my Dad, whose leftwing past made him an excellent target for an ambitious snitch. Strange as it may sound today, tuning in to Deutsche Welle broadcasts became one of a long list of activities punishable by anything from harassment to torture. So, having noticed Gregoris snooping around inside our backyard, my parents took no risks. Thus the red blanket became our defence from Gregoris's prying ears.

A few years later, it was from Deutsche Welle that we learned what Panayiotis and his colleagues had been up to – when the radio announced that they had all been arrested. Dad would joke for years to come about the pathetic inability of these bourgeois liberals to organise an underground resistance group: only a few hours after one of the Democratic Defence members was accidentally caught, the rest were also rounded up. All the police had to do was read the first man's diary – where he had meticulously listed his comrades' names and addresses, in some cases including a description of each subversive 'assignment'. Torture, court martial and long prison sentences – in some cases the death sentence – followed.

A year after Panayiotis's capture, the military police guarding him decided to relax his isolation regime by allowing me, a harmless 10-year-old, to visit him once a week. Our already close bond grew stronger with boy-talk that allowed him a degree of escapism. He told me about machines I had never seen (computers, he called them), asked about the latest movies, described his favourite cars.

In anticipation of my visits, he would use matchsticks and other materials that prison guards would let him keep to build model planes for me. Often, he would hide inside his elegant artefacts a message for my aunt, my mother, on occasion even for his colleagues at Siemens. For my part, I was proud of my new skill of disassembling his models with minimal damage, retrieving the message, and putting them back together.

Long after Panayiotis's death, I discovered the last of these: a matchstick model of a Stuka dive-bomber in my old family home's attic. Torn between leaving it intact and looking inside, I decided to take it apart. And there it was. His last missive was not addressed to anyone in particular.

It was a single word: '*kyriarchia*'. Sovereignty.

It was almost 50 years after those childhood evenings under the red blanket that I made my first official visit to Berlin as finance minister of Greece, in February 2015. My first port of call was, of course, the federal finance ministry, to meet the legendary Dr Wolfgang Schäuble. To him, and his minions, I was a nuisance. Our leftwing government had just been elected, defeating a sister party of the Christian Democrats – New Democracy – on an electoral platform that was, to say the least, a form of inconvenience for Schäuble and Chancellor Angela Merkel, and their plans for keeping the eurozone in order.

Our success was, indeed, Berlin's greatest fear. Were we to succeed in negotiating a new deal for Greece that ended the interminable recession gripping the nation, the Greek leftist 'disease' would almost certainly spread to Portugal, Spain and Ireland, all of which had general elections looming.

Before I arrived in Berlin, and only three days after I had assumed office as minister, I received my first high-ranking visitor in my Athens office: Schäuble's self-appointed envoy, Jeroen Dijsselbloem, the Dutch finance minister and president of the Eurogroup of finance ministers. Within seconds of meeting, he asked me whether I intended to implement fully and unwaveringly the economic programme that previous Greek governments had been forced by Berlin, Brussels and Frankfurt – the seat of the European Central Bank (ECB) – to adopt.

Given that our government had won a mandate to renegotiate the very logic of that disastrous programme (which had led to the loss of one third of national income and increased unemployment by 20%), his question was never going to be the beginning of a beautiful friendship.

For my part, I attempted a diplomatic reply that would be my standard line of argument for the months to follow: 'Given that the existing economic programme has been an indisputable failure, I propose that we sit down together, the new Greek government and our European partners, and rethink the whole programme without prejudice or fear, designing together economic policies that may help Greece recover.'

My modest plea for a modicum of national sovereignty over the economic policies imposed on a nation languishing in the depths of a great depression was met with astonishing brutality. 'This will not work!', was Dijsselbloem's opening line. In less than a minute he had laid his cards on the table: if I were to insist on any substantial renegotiation of the programme, the ECB would close down our banks by the end of February 2015 – a month after we had been elected.

The Greek finance ministry's office overlooks Syntagma Square and the House of Parliament – the very stage on which, in April 1967, the tanks had crushed our democracy. As Dijsselbloem spoke, I caught myself looking over his shoulder out to the broad square teeming with people and thinking to myself: 'This is interesting. In 1967 it was the tanks, now they are trying to do the same with the banks.'

The meeting with Dijsselbloem ended with a tumultuous press conference in which the Eurogroup's president lost his cool when he heard me say that our government was not planning to work with the cabal of technicians the troika of lenders habitually sent to Athens to impose upon the elected government policies destined to fail. The die had been cast and the battle for reclaiming part of our lost sovereignty was only beginning. Berlin, where I was to meet the troika's real master, beckoned.

As the car that was driving me from Berlin's Tegel airport approached the old headquarters of Goering's air ministry –

now the home of the federal ministry of finance – I wondered whether my host, Schäuble, could even begin to imagine that I was arriving in Berlin with my head full of childhood memories in which Germany featured as an important friend.

Once inside the building, my aides and I were ushered briskly into a large lift. The lift door opened up into a long, cold corridor at the end of which awaited the great man in his famous wheelchair. As I approached, my extended hand was refused and, instead of a handshake, he ushered me purposefully into his office.

While my relationship with Schäuble warmed in the months that followed, the shunned hand symbolised a great deal that is wrong with Europe. It was symbolic proof that the half-century that had passed since my red blanket days, and those prison visits to Siemens' man in Athens, had changed Europe to no end.

I have no idea what role Siemens played in securing my uncle's release some time in 1972, two years before the regime's collapse. What I do know is that my parents were convinced that the German company had played a decisive role. For that reason, every time I saw the word 'Siemens' around our home, I felt a warm glow. It is the same kind of warmth I still feel when I hear the words Deutsche Welle. Indeed, back then, in the exciting, bleak years of my childhood, Germany featured in my imagination as a dear friend, a land of democrats that, under Chancellor Willy Brandt, did what was humanly possible to help Greeks rid ourselves of our ugly dictatorship.

Returning home to Athens from my first official visit to Berlin, I was struck by the irony. A continent that had been uniting under different languages and cultures was now divided by a common currency, the euro, and the awful centrifugal forces that it had unleashed throughout Europe.

A week after our first bilateral meeting in Berlin, Schäuble and I were to meet again across the long, rectangular table of the Eurogroup, the eurozone's decision-making body, comprising the common currency's finance ministers, plus the representatives of the troika – the ECB, the European Commission, and the International Monetary Fund. After I had recited our government's plea for a substantial renegotiation of the so-called 'Greek economic programme', which had the troika's fingerprints all over it, Dr Schäuble astounded me with a reply that should send shivers up the spine of every democrat: 'Elections cannot be allowed to change an economic programme of a member state!' he said categorically.

During a break from that 10-hour Eurogroup meeting, in which I had struggled to reclaim some economic sovereignty on behalf of my battered parliament and our suffering people, another finance minister attempted to soothe me by saying: 'Yanis, you must understand that no country can be sovereign today. Especially not a small and bankrupt one like yours.'

This line of argument is probably the most pernicious fallacy to have afflicted public debate in our modern liberal democracies. Indeed, I would go as far as to suggest that it may be the greatest threat to liberal democracy itself. Its true meaning is that sovereignty is passé unless you are the United States, China or, maybe, Putin's Russia. In which case you might as well append your country to a transnational alliance of states where your parliament is reduced to a rubber stamp, and all authority is vested in the larger states.

Interestingly, this argument is not reserved for small, bankrupt countries such as Greece, trapped in a badly designed common currency area. This same noxious dictum is today being peddled in the UK – supposedly as a clinching argument in favour of the remain campaign. As a supporter of Britain remaining in the EU, nothing upsets me more than the enlistment to the 'yes' cause of an argument that is as toxic as it is woolly.

The problem begins once the distinction between sovereignty and power is blurred. Sovereignty is about who decides legitimately on behalf of a people – whereas power is the capacity to impose these decisions on the outside world. Iceland is a tiny country. But to claim that Iceland's sovereignty is illusory because it is too small to have much power is like arguing that a poor person with no political clout might as well give up her right to vote.

To put it slightly differently, small sovereign nations such as Iceland have choices to make within the broader constraints created for them by nature and by the rest of humanity. However limited these choices might be, Iceland's citizens retain absolute authority to hold their elected officials accountable for the decisions they have reached (within the nation's external constraints), and to strike down every piece of legislation those elected officials have decided upon in the past.

An alliance of states, which is what the EU is, can of course come to mutually beneficial arrangements, such as a defensive military alliance against a common aggressor, coordination between police forces, open borders, an agreement to common industry standards, or the creation of a free-trade zone. But it can never legitimately strike down or overrule the sovereignty of one of its member states on the basis of the limited power it has been granted by the sovereign states that have agreed to participate in the alliance. There is no collective European sovereignty from which Brussels could draw the legitimate political authority to do so.

One may retort that the European Union's democratic credentials are beyond reproach. The European Council comprises heads of governments, while Ecofin and the Eurogroup are the councils of finance ministers (of the whole EU and of the eurozone respectively). All these representatives are, of course, democratically elected. Moreover, there is the European parliament, elected by the citizens of the member states, which has the power to send proposed legislation back to the Brussels bureaucracy. But these arguments demonstrate how badly European appreciation of the founding principles of liberal democracy has been degraded. The critical error of such a defence is once more to confuse political authority with power.

A parliament is sovereign, even if its country is not particularly powerful, when it can dismiss the executive for having failed to fulfil the tasks assigned to it within the constraints of whatever power the executive and the parliament possess. Nothing like this exists in the EU today.

For while the members of the European Council and the Eurogroup of finance ministers are elected politicians, answerable, theoretically, to their respective national parliaments, the Council and the Eurogroup are themselves not answerable to any parliament, nor indeed to any voting citizens whatsoever.

Moreover, the Eurogroup, where most of Europe's important economic decisions are taken, is a body that does not even exist in European law, that keeps no minutes of its procedures and insists its deliberations are confidential – that is, not to be shared with the citizens of Europe. It operates on the basis – in the words of Thucydides – that 'strong do as they please while the weak suffer what they must'. It is a set-up designed to preclude any sovereignty derived from the people of Europe.

While opposing Schäuble's logic on Greece in the Eurogroup and elsewhere, at the back of my mind there were two thoughts. First, as the finance minister of a bankrupt state, whose citizens demanded an end to a great depression that had been caused by a denial of our bankruptcy – the imposition of new unpayable loans, so payments could be made on old unpayable loans – I had a political and moral duty to say no to more 'extend-and-pretend' loan agreements. My second thought was the lesson of Sophocles's Antigone, who taught us that good women and men have a duty to contradict rules lacking political and moral legitimacy.

Political authority is the cement that keeps legislation together, and the sovereignty of the body politic that engenders the legislation is its foundation. Saying no to Schäuble and the troika was an essential defence of our right to sovereignty. Not just as Greeks but as Europeans.

How ironic that this should also have been the last missive I received from Siemens' long forgotten man in Athens.

Coming into the highest level of European decision-making from the academic world, where argument and reason are the norm, the most striking realisation was the absence of any meaningful debate. If this was not bad enough, there was an even more painful realisation: that this absence is considered natural – indeed, considered a virtue, and one that newcomers like myself should embrace, or face the consequences.

Prearranged communiques, prefabricated votes, a solid coalition of finance ministers around Schäuble that was impenetrable to rational debate; this was the order to the day and, more often, of the long, long night. Not once did I get the feeling that my interlocutors were at all interested in Greece's economic recovery while we were discussing the economic policies that should be implemented in my country.

From the day I assumed office I strove to put together sensible, moderate proposals that would create common ground between my government, the troika of Greece's lenders and Schäuble's people. The idea was to go to Brussels, put to them our own blueprint for Greece's recovery and then discuss with them their own ideas and objections to ours.

My own Athens-based team worked hard on this, together with experts from abroad, including Jeff Sachs of Columbia University, Thomas Meyer, a former chief economist at Deutsche Bank, Daniel Cohen and Matthieu Pigasse, leading lights of the French investment bank Lazard, the former US treasury secretary Larry Summers, and my personal friend Lord Lamont – not exactly a group of leftist recalcitrants.

Soon we had a fully-fledged plan, whose final version I co-authored with Jeff Sachs. It consisted of three chapters. One proposed smart debt operations that would make Greece's public debt manageable again, while guaranteeing maximum returns to our creditors. The second chapter put forward a medium-term fiscal consolidation policy that would ensure the Greek government would never get into deficit again, while limiting our budget surplus targets to levels low enough to be credible and consistent with recovery. Finally, the third chapter outlined deep reforms to public and tax administration, product markets, and the restructure of a broken banking system as well as the creation of a development bank to manage public assets at an arm's length from politicians.

I am often asked: Why were these proposals of your ministry rejected? They were not. The Eurogroup and the troika did not have to reject them because they never allowed me to put them on the table. When I began speaking about them, they would look at me as if I were singing the Swedish national anthem. And behind the scenes they were exerting pressure on the Greek prime minister, Alexis Tsipras, to repress these proposals, insinuating that there would be no agreement unless we stuck to the troika's failed programme.

What was really going on, of course, was that the troika could simply ignore our proposals, tell the world that I had nothing credible to offer them, let the negotiations fail, impose an indefinite bank holiday, and then force the prime minister to acquiesce on everything – including a massive new loan that is at least double the size Greece would have required under our proposals.

Tragically, despite our prime minister's acceptance of the troika's terms of surrender, and the loss of another year during which Greece's great depression is deepening, the same process is unfolding now. Only a few days ago WikiLeaks revealed the troubling transcript of a telephone conversation involving the International Monetary Fund's participants in the Greek drama. Listening to their discussion confirms that nothing has changed since I resigned last July.

Once I put it to Schäuble that we, as the elected representatives of a continent in crisis, can not defer to unelected bureaucrats; we have a duty to find common ground on the policies that affect people's lives through direct dialogue. He replied that, in his perspective, what matters most is the respect of the existing 'rules'. And since the rules can only be enforced by technocrats, I should talk to them.

Whenever I attempted to discuss rules that were clearly impossible to enforce, the standard reply was: 'But these are the rules!' Once, while I was pushing hard for the argument, resulting from our team's policy work, that primary budget surplus targets of 4.5% of Greece's national income were impossible, and undesirable even from the creditors' perspective, Schäuble looked at me and asked me, perhaps for the first and last time, an economic question. 'So, what would you like that target to be?' At last, I rejoiced, a chance to have a serious discussion.

In an attempt to be as reasonable as possible, I replied: 'For the target of the government budget primary surplus to be credible and realistic, it needs to be consistent with our overall policy mix. The budget surplus number, when added to the difference between savings and investment, must equal Greece's current account balance. Which means that we can strive for a higher budget primary surplus if we also put in place a credible strategy for boosting investment and delivering more credit to exporters.

'So, before I can answer your question, Wolfgang, on what the primary surplus target ought to be, it is crucial that we link this number to our policies on non-performing bank loans (that impede credit to exporters) and investment flows (which are reduced when we set the primary budget surplus target too high, scaring investors off with the implicit threat of higher future taxes). What I can tell you at this point is that the optimal target cannot be more than 1.5%. But let's have our people study this together.'

Schäuble's response to my point, addressing the rest of the Eurogroup while avoiding my eyes, was remarkable: 'The previous government has committed Greece to 4.5% primary surpluses. And a commitment is a commitment!'

A few hours later, the media was full of leaks from the Eurogroup, claiming that 'the Greek finance minister infuriated his colleagues in the Eurogroup by subjecting them to an economics lecture.'

There is a reason why I began this piece with the story of my Uncle Panayiotis. That reason is a question asked by a journalist towards the end of the press conference after my first meeting with Wolfgang Schäuble in Berlin.

The question was about Siemens and a scandal that had broken out some years earlier, when an investigation initiated in the US found evidence that a certain Michalis Christoforakos, a successor of Panayiotis, was actively pushing bribes into the hands of Greek politicians to secure government contracts on behalf of Siemens. Soon after the Greek authorities began investigating the matter, the gentleman absconded to Germany, where the courts prevented his extradition to Athens.

'Did you, minister,' asked the journalist, 'impress upon your German colleague' – that would be Wolfgang Schäuble – 'the German state's obligation to help the Greek government snuff out corruption by extraditing Mr Christoforakos to Greece?' I tried to honour the question with a reasonable answer. 'I am sure,' I said, 'that the German authorities will understand the importance of assisting our troubled state in its struggle against corruption in Greece. I trust that my colleagues in Germany understand the importance of not being seen to have double standards anywhere in Europe.' Looking terribly put out, Schäuble mumbled that this was not a matter for his finance ministry.

On the aeroplane back to Athens, my mind travelled to the late 1970s. After his release from prison, Panayiotis returned to the helm of Siemens Greece. He was happy in that job, as he kept telling me, and proud of his work. Until he stopped being proud of it – so much so that he resigned in anger.

I remember asking him why he had resigned. His answer still resonates. He told me that he was facing pressure from his superiors in Germany to pay bribes to Greek politicians to ensure that Siemens would maintain its dominant position in Greece, getting the lion's share of contracts related to the lucrative digitisation of the Greek telephone network.

There is a touching faith in the European north that Europe

comprises ants and grasshoppers – and that all the frugal and cautious ants live in the north, while the spendthrift grasshoppers have congregated mysteriously in the south. The reality is much more muddled. A mighty network of corrupt practices has been laid over all of our countries – and the collapse of democratic checks and balances, due in part to our receding sovereignty, has helped hide it from public view.

As legitimate political authority retreats, we fall in the lap of brute force, inertia and demonisation of the weak. Indeed, by the end of June 2015, the ECB had shut our banks, our government was divided, I resigned my ministry, and my prime minister capitulated to the troika.

The crushing of the Athens spring was a serious blow for an already wounded Greece. But it was also a wholesale defeat for the idea of a united, humanist, democratic Europe.

Our European Union is disintegrating. Should we accelerate the disintegration of a failed confederacy? If one insists that even small countries can retain their sovereignty, as I have done, does this mean Brexit is the obvious course? My answer is an emphatic 'No!'

Here is why: if Britain and Greece were not already in the EU, they should most certainly stay out. But, once inside, it is crucial to consider the consequences of a decision to leave. Whether we like it or not, the European Union is our environment – and it has become a terribly unstable environment, which will disintegrate even if a small, depressed country like Greece leaves, let alone a major economy like Britain. Should the Greeks or the Brits care about the disintegration of an infuriating EU? Yes, of course we should care. And we should care very much because the disintegration of this frustrating alliance will create a vortex that will consume us all – a postmodern replay of the 1930s.

It is a major error to assume, whether you are a remain or a leave supporter, that the EU is something constant 'out there' that you may or may not want to be part of. The EU's very existence depends on Britain staying in. Greece and Britain are facing the same three options. The first two are represented aptly by the two warring factions within the Tory party: deference to Brussels and exit. They are equally calamitous options. Both lead to the same dystopian future: a Europe fit only for those who flourish in times of a great Depression – the xenophobes, the ultra-nationalists, the enemies of democratic sovereignty. The third option is the only one worth going for: staying in the EU to form a cross-border alliance of democrats, which Europeans failed to manage in the 1930s, but which our generation must now attempt to prevent history repeating itself.

This is precisely what some of us are working towards in creating DiEM25 – the Democracy in Europe Movement, with a view to conjuring up a democratic surge across Europe, a common European identity, an authentic European sovereignty, an internationalist bulwark against both submission to Brussels and hyper-nationalist reaction.

Is this not utopian? Of course it is! But not more so than the notion that the current EU can survive its anti-democratic hubris, and the gross incompetence fuelled by its unaccountability. Or the idea that British or Greek democracy can be revived in the bosom of a nation-state whose sovereignty will never be restored within a single market controlled by Brussels.

Just like in the early 1930s, Britain and Greece cannot escape Europe by building a mental or legislative wall behind which to hide. Either we band together to democratise – or we suffer the consequences of a pan-European nightmare that no border can keep out.

Yanis Varoufakis is a Greek economist, academic and politician, who served as Minister of Finance in the Syriza government from January to July 2015.

Defending our rights: rising to the challenge of Brexit Britain

CAROLINE LUCAS

On the morning of 24th June, after hearing the final result of the referendum while in a BBC studio at Millbank, I walked onto Westminster Bridge and looked back at the House of Commons which was glowing in the dawn sunshine. I knew then that everything would be different, and that Britain would be entering tough times. But I didn't anticipate just how swiftly the Tories would align themselves with the braying right-wing press and reframe this narrow victory to leave the EU as an overwhelming majority in favour of leaving everything, including the Single Market.

The left should be under no illusions about the scale of the crisis we face. After a rancorous referendum campaign which saw us drowned out of a battle raging on the airwaves between an increasingly out of touch political elite and the rising power of the so-called anti-establishment right, we've been left bruised, battered and sidelined when it comes to Europe.

At this stage in proceedings it's easy to look back bitterly on the campaign, and blame others for our failings. There's no doubt that the media latched onto the 'fight on the right' and particularly wanted to paint the 'remain' case as that of the

Prime Minister and his allies. Some on our own side didn't help either – as they persistently made a half-baked case for staying in the EU, despite many of us warning of the darkness around the corner if we left. Of particular frustration was the unwillingness of some at the top of the Labour Party (with notable exceptions) to work across party lines with the SNP, Plaid Cymru and the Green Party in making a targeted anti-establishment case for remaining a member of the world's most successful peace project, and reforming it to make it work better.

But the truth is that all of us could and should have done more to keep Britain in the EU, and we probably would have if we'd known just how challenging the political climate would be in the first few months of post-referendum Britain. Not only are we facing economic uncertainty, but people who have come to Britain to live and work are being subjected to regular doses of toxic rhetoric on migration from government ministers.

We now face a Conservative government which is treating the referendum result as carte blanche for remodelling Britain in the way they see fit, rather than using this as the springboard for the democratic revolution we so desperately need. Instead of taking the opportunity to negotiate the future with the British public, May looks set to impose her own ideologically-driven 'hard Brexit' and that means Britain leaving the Single Market. Not only does such a choice mean scrapping our trade relationship with our biggest trading partner, it also risks tearing up crucial environmental and social protections which come as part of the package. Moreover, May's timetable means we also face the seemingly impossible task of completing what are usually seven-year trade deal negotiations in just two years.

Amid such chaos it is clear that we desperately need a cohesive, progressive vision for Britain's relationship with Europe.

For us, as the Green Party, that vision rests upon four crucial pillars: retaining free movement, protecting our environment, safeguarding social rights and reimagining our democracy.

We all know that the government is insistent about its intention to end free movement between Britain and the rest of Europe. Such a move risks further dividing our communities and sending deeply worrying signals to our neighbours, friends, family and work colleagues with whom we live side by side. Britain's reputation as a tolerant, diverse country is under threat. Ending free movement would also hit us hard economically because EU nationals who come here pay far more into the exchequer than they take out – giving our public services a boost and supporting our ageing society. It also threatens our universities, limits the prospects of young people living abroad and, according to some businesses in my city, Brighton and Hove, leaves them with a skill shortage too. It's particularly outrageous that the government still hasn't given a guarantee to EU nationals living here now that they will have a guaranteed right to remain in the UK.

Our environmental protections are under threat too. As a recent Environmental Audit Committee report noted: 'There are few areas of Government policy where the decision to leave the European Union will have a more widespread impact.' While the government claims that its 'Great Repeal Bill' will enshrine EU environmental protections into law, we know that this is far from a guaranteed safeguard. Two major uncertainties around environmental safeguards exist. The first is that upon exiting the EU, Britain can amend or repeal any aspects of environmental legislation that it chooses, subject to appropriate Parliamentary scrutiny.

Secondly, and perhaps more immediately concerning, is the fact that by leaving the EU Britain would no longer be accountable to the institutions which monitor and enforce implementation of environmental laws. At present, the UK is required to report periodically (and publicly) to the European Commission on the implementation of EU laws such as the Birds and Habitats Directives. These mechanisms are critical in terms of transparently assessing progress. Once the UK leaves the EU these obligations will cease to apply, and the European Commission will cease to be responsible for monitoring and enforcing compliance, potentially resulting in less robust enforcement mechanisms and considerable governance/accountability gaps compared to the status quo. In addition, the important role played by the Commission in helping to coordinate action across member states and facilitating the sharing of expertise may be lost. Furthermore, the European Court of Justice will no longer have jurisdiction here in Britain – thus rendering many crucial protections unenforceable.

Though the threat to our environmental laws from Brexit is particularly acute we should also be aware of what a post-referendum Britain could look like for hard-won social protections. The government appears to have ruled out any immediate attack on workers' rights but, as Britain re-negotiates its place in the world, there is a distinct threat of our country being remodelled as a low wage 'open' economy undercutting its European neighbours. You only have to look at the damaging Trade Union Bill to get a sense of the government's intentions when it comes to industrial relations. While EU rules protect citizens from across the continent from a race to the bottom on rights at work, our government will be freed from any such responsibility.

With the UK facing such grave, even existential, threats it would be easy for the left to wither. But, instead, we must rise to the challenge.

That's why, in defence of free movement, environmental protections and workers' rights we are arguing that Britain should remain a member of the Single Market. We must not pretend that this is a perfect solution – it would leave us with a democratic deficit because we'd no longer have MEPs representing us in Brussels, or a seat at the top table – but with the British government steadfastly refusing to allow the British people any meaningful say in the post-referendum period we believe it's the best way to protect ourselves from the serious dangers of a hard Brexit. If the government does take us out of the Single Market then it will be down to progressives of all hues to work together at every step of the way to protect the laws and freedoms which we hold dear.

Staying in the Single Market or fighting against the repeal of social and environmental protections, are defensive moves against a reactionary government, and they must be matched with a proactive commitment to genuine democracy. It is abundantly clear from the referendum that people are sick and tired of being pushed out of politics, and having decisions made for them. That's why, if we're serious about allowing people to 'take back control' we need to give them a further say on the terms of any deal and allow MPs to properly scrutinise the decision-making process and vote before the triggering of Article 50. We also need a Great Reform Bill which would update British democracy for the twenty-first century and hand real power to people in the form of a fair voting system for both the House of Commons and the House of Lords.

The truth is that the result of the referendum has left me feeling torn. On the one hand, as a democrat and as someone who believes in giving people more power, I accept that the British people made this choice on 23 June. But on the other hand, as an MP elected to stand up for what I believe in – for social, economic and environmental justice – I find the prospect of Brexit genuinely frightening. It is my belief that Britain would be better off if we stayed in the EU – and that my constituents face real risks as a result of us leaving.

The Green Party will not be seeking to ride roughshod over the decision we took as a country on 23 June 2016. Instead we will be advocating for democracy to remain the top priority, and for workers, our environment and free movement to be protected in any Brexit deal. We won't sit back and watch while the Conservatives use this as an opportunity to fashion a Britain whose place in the world is as a free-market tax haven on the edge of Europe, defined in stature by the size of our nuclear arsenal and locked behind hard borders and wire fences.

Some might call what we're pursuing 'soft Brexit' – I call it our best hope of easing the pain of leaving the European Union. Of course we would want Britain to remain a member of the world's most successful peace project and will be doing all we can to continue to make the case for co-operation with our neighbours. But it would be irresponsible not to engage in this new uncertain reality, which otherwise will solely be determined by the men that one of my fellow Remain campaigners dubbed the Eton mess. I am in no doubt that, if that clique is left to its own devices, Britain will be sold short. I am not prepared to stand by and let that happen. Not prepared to see the principle that lies behind taking back control turned on itself and used as an excuse to trample over hard won rights, making us a smaller, narrower nation. If the EU referendum campaign taught us anything it's that the truth's precious and, as we struggle to find a way through the uncertainty of the coming months and years, perhaps the most important thing any of us can do is speak truth to power.

Caroline Lucas is the co-leader of the Green Party and MP for Brighton Pavilion.

Taking back control through Europe: the example of European security policy

MARY KALDOR

Four days after the British referendum on membership of the European Union, the High Representative for Common Foreign and Security Policy, Federica Mogherini, presented a new document to the European Council entitled *Shared Vision, Common Action: A Stronger Europe: A Global Strategy for the European Union's Foreign and Security Policy.*[1] The report was the outcome of a two year-process with widespread consultation both among governments and among experts, think tanks, universities and relevant NGOs. The report represents a stark contrast to the typical national strategy reviews that are put forward by national governments. There is almost no mention of 'threats' and although the report favours a more integrated defence sector, this constitutes a very minor part of the overall strategy. The word 'global' refers both to the world context and, at the same time, to the array of instruments and issues that such a strategy must address. Par-

---

1. https://europa.eu/globalstrategy/en/global-strategy-foreign-and-security-policy-european-union

ticularly interesting is the concern with regional organisations like the EU as forms of global governance. The main thrust of the report is the commitment to citizens, the blurring of the distinction between inside and outside, and the importance of common action. In her foreword, Mogherini points out that the Union faces an existential crisis. In other words, the report is about the security of citizens rather than the state and this depends on being united, acting together and reaching out beyond the continent rather than defending borders in a traditional way.

A year earlier, at the June 2015 EU Summit, Mogherini presented a document, *The European Union in a changing global environment: A more connected, contested and complex world,*[2] that provides the foundation for the *Global Strategy*. It explained why classic intergovernmental institutions are no longer fit for purpose; it argued that concepts like 'borders' and 'polarity' no longer capture reality and that the EU represents a new meaning of power that no longer 'resides within actors but circulates among them'; it talked about a world of mobility and a world that is 'complex, contested and connected'.

What never seems to have been discussed in the debate leading up to the referendum and indeed since then is the nature of the EU as an institution that is illustrated by the *Global Strategy*. In this essay I argue that the EU has to be understood as a new type of political institution that offers the only possibility for citizens to 'take back control' in the context of the phenomenon we call globalisation and I use the example of security policy, especially the policy towards conflict, to illustrate what I mean. The EU is not a super-state, as Boris Johnson and other Brexiteers claim. But nor is it a classic inter-governmental organisation since it involves majority voting on many issues and a much denser set of interconnections than most inter-governmental institutions. It is better understood as a new twenty-first century type of political institution – a model of global gov-

---

2. https://europa.eu/globalstrategy/en/european-union-changing-global-environment

ernance, perhaps, that has the capacity, even if not or not much currently used, to address global challenges like financial speculation, climate change or war so as to protect local autonomy.

I start with a description of the EU as a new form of political authority. I then use the example of EU policy towards conflict as an illustration. I then sketch the evolution of the EU and the tensions it currently faces. And I conclude by speculating on the dangers of being stuck as a consequence of Brexit in twentieth-century ways of doing things.

THE EU AS A NEW FORM OF POLITICAL AUTHORITY

The European project after World War Two was a peace project. In the eighteenth and nineteenth centuries, many great philosophers developed perpetual peace schemes – Jean-Jacques Rousseau, Immanuel Kant, and John Stuart Mill. The founders of the EU wanted to prevent the recurrence of the absolutist twentieth-century tragedies. In many ways, the construction of the EU bears resemblance to the Kantian scheme, which involved a combination of a permanent peace treaty, republican (or formally democratic) constitutions, and cosmopolitan rights (e.g. human rights). This scheme is not the construction of a super-state like the United States, for example. Rather it is a new form of supranational co-operation, which restrains the worst characteristics of the nation-state – war, imperialism and repression.

This peace project should be contrasted with the European nation-state project that was founded on war; Charles Tilly has shown that it was through war against other states that the institutions and relations of statehood were established.[3] As Tilly himself put it: 'War made the State and States made war'.[4]

Because it began as a peace project and has developed through agreements and treaties in a globalizing context, it can

---

3. Charles Tilly, *Coercion, Capital and European States, AD 990-1992*, Blackwell, 1993.

4. Ibid.

be argued that the EU represents a different conception of power. The nation-state was the typical political form of the twentieth century. It could be described as the archetypal example of a 'modern' institution, characterised by binary distinctions and a range of methods for compartmentalising and categorising various aspects of society and geography. Twentieth-century nation-states involved a sharp distinction between 'inside' and 'outside' power. Outside power, as International Relations scholars explain, was based on national attributes of power such as economic wealth, military strength, or communicative capabilities – Joseph Nye's notion of 'hard' and 'soft' power.[5] Inside power was based on politics, law and legitimacy. In the context of globalisation (interconnectedness in all fields), it is no longer possible to sustain that distinction. The EU acts more like an inside power, not only in terms of the relations among its members, but also in its relations with the rest of the world, especially its neighbours.

EU SECURITY POLICY
This different conception of power is very well illustrated by EU security policy, especially the strategy towards conflict. Armed conflict is the sharp edge of contemporary crises. No country can insulate itself from the knock-on effects of armed conflict, whether we are talking about forced displacement and the refugee crisis, organised crime and its link to offshore companies and money laundering, including through property prices, or polarisation around extremist, misogynist and/or homophobic identity politics. Yet classic twentieth-century national approaches (military intervention or top-down diplomacy or doing nothing) do not work and make things worse. From Turkey to Syria and Yemen, from Afghanistan to Burma or the Philippines, from the Horn of Africa to the Democratic Republic of Congo, not to mention Colombia or Mexico and Venezuela, or

---

5. Joseph Nye, *The Future of Power, Public Affairs*, 2011

Ukraine and the Caucasus, the world seems to be facing a series of intractable spreading conflicts.

It was not until 2000 that the EU established a security policy. Soon after the war, the vexing question of whether Germany and Italy should be allowed to re-establish armed forces was raised. The main proposal was to integrate these two countries into a European Defence Community. This proposal was voted down, however, in the French National Assembly in 1954 by a combination of leftists who opposed rearmament, and nationalists. Instead the West European Union was established – basically composed of the European members of NATO. It was the WEU that was later merged into the European Security and Defence Policy (ESD), now the Common Security and Defence Policy.

The first High Representative for Common Foreign and Security Policy was Javier Solana. The post was created in order to answer Kissinger's question about who to telephone for Europe. It coincided with the decision taken after a meeting between Tony Blair and Jacques Chirac in St Malo in December 1998 to establish a European Security and Defence Policy (ESDP) in order to be able to act autonomously from the United States. From the beginning ESDP had a distinct philosophy from national security policy. It was not about military defence of borders; rather it was about the so-called St Petersburg tasks – these include humanitarian and rescue tasks, peace-keeping and crisis management,[6] that is to say tasks relating primarily to conflict.

Since the establishment of the Common Security and Defence Policy (CSDP), there have been over 30 missions under UN mandates both civilian and military aimed at preventing atrocities, public security especially during elections, establishing a rule of law, anti-piracy and humanitarian missions. The EU is the biggest aid donor in the world and this includes, for

---

6. They are called the St Petersburg tasks because they were defined at a meeting of the WEU in St Petersburg in 1992.

example, the financing of the Palestinian Authority. The plethora of association and membership agreements about such issues as trade, dialogue and human rights can be regarded as mechanisms for spreading the inside outside.

This is not to say that EU policies are effective; indeed they are very imperfect. I use the term 'hybrid peace' to describe what happens when twentieth-century methods of peace-making are applied in twenty-first century conflict contexts.[7] EU policies towards conflict are mostly directed at stabilisation on classic peace-making lines; they involve the provision of humanitarian assistance, mediation among the warring parties, and 'post-conflict' reconstruction. Where the warring parties are extremist criminalised groups, such policies are easily subverted. Humanitarian assistance is channelled into a predatory war economy; top-down mediation ends up entrenching the positions of the warring parties; and reconstruction provides further opportunities for those parties to enrich themselves at the expense of ordinary citizens. While hybrid peace may be preferable to hybrid war or the War on Terror, nevertheless these situations are characterised by continuing crime, human rights violations and the ever present danger of reverting to war. EU missions and programmes are also weakened by lack of political backing both nationally and EU-wide, as well as by increasingly muscular counter-terror policies adopted at national levels and by the United States and the reversion to geo-politics embraced by nation-states and NATO.

One of the most interesting parts of the *Global Strategy* is the section on conflicts and crises where it explicitly recognises some of these problems. It calls for an integrated approach based on human security that is multi-dimensional, multi-level and multi-lateral. It puts emphasis on inclusive political set-

---

7. See *From Hybrid Peace to Human Security: Rethinking EU Strategy towards Conflict: the Berlin report of the Human Security Study Group*, http://www.securityintransition.org/publications/berlin-report-of-the-human-security-study-group/

tlements, on gender, and, above all, on the need to reverse the political economy of conflicts and establish 'legitimate econo- mies'. Potentially, it constitutes the building blocks of a different approach but it may remain no more than a paper narrative – something we may look back on as an interesting counter fac- tual if the European experiment fails.

THE EVOLUTION OF THE EUROPEAN PROJECT

The main method through which the EU was constructed was economic. The founders of the EU thought that through what was known as 'low politics', 'high politics' would follow – this was the so-called Monnet method named after the French politician Jean Monnet. For the first three decades, the Mon- net method seemed to work; it involved co-operation on infra- structure, agriculture and regional assistance. But everything changed after 1989. This was the heyday of the post-1968 so- cial movements – what we might call the cosmopolitans, who favoured peace and human rights and who wanted to end the Cold War division of Europe. But it was also the heyday of a new generation of neo-liberals, who made use of the left critique of the paternalism and rigidity of the nation-state. The 1991 Maastricht Treaty, which established the single market and the common currency, was a compromise between the cosmopoli- tans and the neo-liberals, between the passionate Europeanism of Jacques Delors, then the President of the European Commis- sion, and the neo-liberalism of Margaret Thatcher.

Many argued that the single currency was a mistake. To es- tablish a single currency without a large central budget, with- out a fiscal union (for taxation and spending) and without a political union was bound to lead to deep inequalities between creditor and debtor nations. But the late Ulrich Beck pointed out that it was not a mistake; it was a deliberate continuation of the Monnet method. Precisely because it was an impossible project, it created a vested interest in political union. In other words those who agreed to the common currency knew that the project would propel further integration. And this is where we are now.

On the one hand, true to the cosmopolitanism of the founders, the EU has made considerable strides in establishing rights, including freedom of movement, environmental protections, new mechanisms for transnational democracy such as the European Citizens Initiative, as well as a rights-based external policy such as the policy on conflicts. On the other hand, the austerity policies associated with the single currency have created social exclusion, fragmentation and atomisation, which in turn has given rise to right-wing populism across Europe, dangerously expressed in the Brexit vote, even though this was due to the ideology of the Conservative government and not the single currency.

This is why the EU has reached the point where low politics has to be translated into high politics. Europe has to go forward to survive. It has to integrate further. It has to act as a twenty-first century institution. It has to reverse the rules about austerity and introduce a fiscal policy that includes the regulation of financial speculation and the closure of multinational tax havens. It has to manage the migration crisis, not make things worse through border controls that merely increase the dangers to those fleeing war and poverty. It has to promote green and socially just economic development. And it has to adopt a serious strategy towards conflict.

The alternative is dangerous disintegration. Brexit is just the beginning. Because none of these problems can be solved at a national level and certainly not through classic national methods, Brexit will be very bad for Britain, making us poorer, more polarised, and less able to control our lives. It is possible that Europeans will react to Brexit by taking the necessary steps to integrate further. But it is also possible that the societal waves of distrust and fear associated with Brexit and shared across the continent will be hard to contain.

A DIFFERENT EUROPE

The aim of the European project should be to 'take back control'. The aim is to make it possible for individual citizens to influence the decisions that affect their lives. This cannot be achieved through building a European super-state and all that goes with it – surveillance, borders and a military-industrial complex. Rather Europe has to become a new regional model of global governance – not an instrument of globalisation as it is now, but a mechanism for taming globalisation, for protecting local levels from the storms of globalisation. Europe has to restrain global bads like financial speculation or climate change, and promote global goods like solidarity, peace and human rights in our neighbourhood and beyond. This might be expressed in a new sort of fiscal union, with a new set of taxes aimed at global bads, like a tax on financial speculation or on carbon, and spending on global goods, like resource-saving innovation, youth employment, peace-building or redistribution. The policy towards conflict discussed above is an illustration of this kind of twenty-first century approach

The *Global Strategy* makes the case for regional ordering of the world:

'Voluntary forms of regional governance offer states and peoples the opportunity to better manage security concerns, reap the economic gains of globalisation, express more fully cultures and identities, and project influence in world affairs. This is a fundamental rationale for the EU's own peace and development in the 21st century. This is why we will promote and support cooperative regional orders worldwide, including in the most divided areas. . . We will not strive to export our model, but rather seek reciprocal inspiration from different regional experiences.'

Leaving the EU will leave us in the UK caught in twentieth-century understandings and practices that no longer work in our globalised context and, indeed, backfire and make things worse especially if what we get is a 'hard' Brexit. Tightening borders will merely increase the dangers for migrants; criminals and terrorists who are supposed to be excluded will always find ways to circumvent borders. Air strikes against terrorists merely provoke more attacks in Europe. Arming against foreign 'threats' like Russia and China will result in a dangerous arms race and encourage the proliferation of weapons. The EU, for all its imperfections, is the only alternative to being stuck in twentieth-century ways of doing things.

That is why as part of our campaigning to prevent the worst outcome of the referendum, we need to co-operate with others in Europe who want to save the European peace project and promote human security. Even if we are not members of the EU, we remain part of Europe and the future of the Union matters for us.

Mary Kaldor is Professor of Global Governance at the London School of Economics, where she is also the Director of the Civil Society and Human Security Research Unit.

Brexit and the democratic deficit

MARINA PRENTOULIS

The discussion over the democratic deficit of the EU has been around for a long time. Originally it referred to the transfer of powers from the national level to the EU institutions and later to the balancing of power between a 'union of nations', a 'union of citizens' and a 'union of people', aiming to create the conditions where no nation would be a lesser partner and no citizen powerless. In the last few years, following the financial crisis of 2007-8, it has become apparent that the EU has failed on all those counts. The 'union of nations' is regressing to divisions and nationalisms with some citizens enjoying full rights while others see their rights stripped away. The collective wellbeing of the peoples of the EU is excluded from institutional considerations and overlooked for the benefit of global corporate and financial interests. Key moments exposing how far the EU has derailed from its social vision are the 2015 negotiations between the Greek government and the Troika (IMF, EC, ECB), and the British referendum in June 2016.

When the negotiations between the EU institutions, the IMF and the Greek government started in the summer of 2015, it became obvious once more that the crisis would be employed as a moralising mechanism to punish states, citizens and people already badly hit by it, overwhelmingly in the south of Europe.

Already in the spring of 2010, Greece, unable to service its loans, had been subjected to lending programmes (memoranda) that enforced severe austerity on the country and worsened its already huge debt. The haircut of the Greek debt in 2012 (primarily towards private lenders such as banks, insurance companies and investment companies) did not deliver the reduction from 160% of GDP to 120% (for the period 2011-2020) that was promised. Instead the debt continued to increase (reaching around 180% of GDP), and successive austerity policies led to the disintegration of the social fabric of the country. By January 2015 when the anti-austerity government of SYRIZA (Coalition of the Radical Left)-ANEL (Independent Greeks) came to power, the situation in Greece was critical; the reduction in pensions and wages had reached 40%, one in four was out of work and youth unemployment had reached 60%. Almost four million people living in Greece – more than a third of the country's total population – were classed as being 'at risk of poverty or social exclusion'.[1]

The Greek negotiations achieved something that in a way mirrors the British referendum. They allowed the 'people' to invade the central stage in politics.

We should not forget that SYRIZA came to power in 2015 after drawing electoral support from the movement of the squares in Greece (2011). This was rendered possible by connecting the diverse, heterogeneous demands of the protests in a programme that promised to eliminate the humanitarian crisis, freeze private debt that exceeded one third of the income of each household, restructure the state and finally, revitalize the economy through the strengthening of labour rights[2]. SYRIZA's negotiations in 2015 were aimed at putting an end to the

1. Lucy Rodgers & Nassos Stylianou, 'How bad are things for the people of Greece', http://www.bbc.co.uk/news/world-europe-33507802, accessed 18/10/16.

2. Institute Rosa Luxemburg (2015), *5 Years of Crisis*, Brussels & Athens (in Greek).

demand of primary surpluses, writing off part of the debt and ending the politics of austerity. As the negotiations progressed, it became clear that there was no appetite for any of these demands, as they could send the wrong signal across Europe: a U-turn on austerity policies.

Soon the negotiations reached an impasse and the lenders issued an ultimatum to the Greek government on 29 June 2015. The Greek government's appeal to the European Stability Mechanism (ESM) to provide liquidity to the Greek banks was also rejected,[3] and capital controls were put into effect, a move perceived as a cynical attempt by the EU institutions to pressure Greece into submission. At this point, the Greek government evoked the only possible tool available to resist the demands of the EU institutions: namely the democratic mandate of the people and called for a referendum on 5 July 2015. To the surprise of many in Europe, the Greek people voted for the rejection of the lending agreement enforcing the continuation of austerity (with a majority of almost 62% of the vote). The outcome of the referendum was rejected by the Troika and another memorandum enforcing yet more structural adjustments and austerity was forced upon Greece. The rejection of the democratic mandate of the Greek people is a stain that will haunt the EU for a long time and the beginning of a series of rejections by the peoples of Europe of what is perceived as a highly undemocratic union.

The negotiations dominated the media agenda of most European countries for months on end, including Britain. Rarely do the EU processes become so newsworthy and offer so much drama that speaks directly to all social strata in society. Complex economic and political processes, however, offered the opportunity for a simplistic narrative allowing prejudices to crystallize while leaving structural deficiencies of the European

---

3. The ECB refused the National Bank of Greece's appeal to the European Stability Mechanism, resulting in the end of liquidity for Greece.

Union and particularly the Eurozone, to go unchallenged. The opportunity for a robust critique of global neoliberal structures was missed.

A large part of the British media output could be summarized as occupying two dominant positions: either allying with EU and German spokespersons in order to justify the imposition of neoliberal austerity (domestically and in Greece) or being more sympathetic to the Greek case against what was perceived as the tyranny of the undemocratic EU – this latter fitted comfortably within the widespread Eurosceptic discourse in the UK. It is true that the critique of neoliberal economics and austerity as employed in Greece resonated with the experience of austerity in Britain and was welcomed by the left. But we should emphasise the fact that it also assisted the rejection of the EU driven by conservative forces in the UK. While in Greece after years of austerity and grassroots struggles a left-leaning narrative had become dominant, in Britain the dominant frame is still being shaped by the right. This domination of the right and extreme right in both the Remain and the Leave camps was evident during the referendum. More nuanced arguments advanced by the left during the EU referendum campaign never received much publicity and even when they did, they were not given the time and space necessary to challenge the dominant discourse. These arguments recognise the complexity of the situation. On the one hand, they acknowledge the domination of EU institutions by neoliberal forces, which refused to remedy the structural deficiencies of the financial and banking sectors and were willing to sacrifice democratic accountability in order to protect global capital; on the other hand they suggest that the EU could still be stirred towards a social or even socialist future, by electing left-leaning national governments supported by dynamic social movements across Europe, shifting the balance of power in the EU institutions.

Although there are significant differences between the British and Greek referenda, both have in common the rejection of the European elites, perceived as distant, undemocratic and indifferent to the people of Europe. What the British establishment managed to achieve, however, (both in its Remain and Leave expression) was the disconnection between the conservative neoliberal agenda, pursued by successive governments since the 1980s at the domestic and EU level, and its role in the domination of this agenda at EU level. Instead, the EU was demonized for domestic failures and a powerful new conservative vision emerged victorious from this process, a vision that offers little comfort both to EU nationals residing in the UK and the most vulnerable of British nationals alike.

Unquestionably, the dominant topics during the Leave campaign were immigration and the fiscal burden of EU membership. According to the latest research by the University of Warwick, the 'results highlight that policy choices related to pressure from immigration, fiscal cuts and the housing market are linked to a higher Vote Leave share, especially when socio-economic fundamentals are "weak" (low incomes, high unemployment), and when the local population is less able to adapt to adverse shocks (due to low qualifications and a rising age profile)' [4]. In other words, those affected most by the austerity of the Cameron government could translate EU migration into a cause of their situation. The study also concludes that the 'results indicate that modest reductions in fiscal cuts could have swayed the referendum outcome' [5].

But while the demonization of EU immigration framed the

---

4. Becker, O. S., Fetzer, T., Novy, D. (2016) *Who Voted for Brexit*, Warwick, p.4 http://www2.warwick.ac.uk/fac/soc/economics/research/centres/cage/manage/publications/305-2016_becker_fetzer_novy.pdf, (accessed 18/10/16).

5. Becker, O. S., Fetzer, T., Novy, D. (2016), *Who Voted for Brexit*, Warwick, p. 1 http://www2.warwick.ac.uk/fac/soc/economics/research/centres/cage/manage/publications/305-2016_becker_fetzer_novy.pdf (accessed 18/10/16).

whole referendum debate, austerity did not feature in it. Instead the rhetoric of 'taking back control' and the democratic deficit of the EU helped to derail the debate from questions over the relationship between neoliberalism and democracy, at national and European levels. This has not been the case in Greece where already since the movement of the squares in 2011 both national and European elites have been condemned as undemocratic in their servitude to neoliberalism.

The delusionary nature of the Leave vote and the way in which the focus on the democratic deficit of the EU eradicated any criticism of the undemocratic structures and policy orientation of the UK is evident around the debate on trade agreements.

For the past few years, the EU has been trying to agree on two trade deals, one with the US, the Transatlantic Trade and Investment Partnership (TTIP), and one with Canada, the Comprehensive Economic and Trade Agreement (CETA). The details of the deals promoting trade and multilateral economic growth have been kept classified from the public but multiple leaks have brought to light information that has caused widespread controversy and opposition to the deals by unions, NGOs, and activists. The finalization of TTIP, which was planned for the end of 2014, has fallen through and CETA has recently been rejected by the Belgian regional government (Wallonia) through a resolution requiring the unanimous agreement of all 28 EU member states.

One of the points of contestation regarding both deals is the introduction of Investment-State Dispute Settlement (ISDS) 'courts', composed of corporate lawyers rather than judges, enabling American and Canadian corporations to sue governments, if they see their profits threatened. While many naively believed that after Brexit these deals would not apply to Britain, it was little discussed during the campaign that the UK government was one of the most dedicated supporters of these deals and that it chose to include the NHS in these deals in the first place. Worse, these deals including the ISDS system, if they come through, will become the template for other trade deals (bilateral deals that will shape the future of the UK outside the EU as well).

Comparing the UK with the EU, one could suggest that the former allows less democratic accountability and transparency than the EU transnational institutions, despite their flaws. Unelected bodies like the House of Lords; an electoral system of 'first past the post'; and the medieval structure of the Corporation of London – the local council responsible for the Square Mile where votes rest with the largest corporations ensuring that the interests of the City are protected in Parliament[6] – speak volumes of the state of UK democracy. And yet none of these issues caused concern during the referendum campaign.

AFTER THE BREXIT VOTE

Already since the start of the prolonged period that will define the future relationship between Britain and the EU, there has been a demand that the democratic processes for achieving this new relationship should begin with accountability, transparency and participation at national level. In Britain a new discourse redefining citizenship and rights is in the making with Theresa May's government.

The marked shift in the conservative political rhetoric, situated somewhere between 'Blue Labour' and 'Red Toryism', is already promising to deal with the contradictions of neoliberalism, creating a more 'homogeneous' dystopian narrative. This emerging discourse is constructed around new exclusions and simultaneously ring-fences and limits notions of 'rights'. It rests on the creation of new divisions and exclusions around citizenship. Apart from leaving three million EU citizens in limbo, viewing them as a mere negotiating card, it redefines who the

---

6. George Monbiot, 'The medieval, unaccountable Corporation of London is ripe for protest', *Guardian*, 31/10/11.

state should 'look after'. It follows that this new discourse develops a new type of protective state. As it has been argued, 'the state that looks after people (its *own* people) is not quite the same as the state that *cares* for people, of the sort that was developed in Britain after World War Two. If May wanted to push care to the centre of her vision, this would mean a new politics of welfare, one which used fiscal policy to respond to basic social and physical needs. Needs are things we all have by virtue of our humanity, not our identity'.[7] What we are ending up with is a prejudicial state that will knit together the national, the economic and the cultural.

Within this new construction, the Tory government has to 'look after its people' by closing down democratic discussion and participation over the still unknown content of 'Brexit' (which means 'Brexit' in a tautological trope that shuts down discussion on concrete contents). The debates around who can trigger Article 50 and the repeal of the European Communities Act 1972 before the UK has agreed the terms for its EU departure, reducing drastically the ability of the MPs to challenge the terms of Brexit, is the new battleground for the democratization of British society. These are the issues around which the future of UK democracy rests.

Marina Prentoulis is Senior Lecturer in Media and Politics at the University of East Anglia and a spokesperson for the *Another Europe is Possible* campaign.

---

7. Davies, W (2016), 'The Protective State', http://www.perc.org.uk/project_posts/the-protective-state/, accessed 18/10/16.

Oppose Little Brexit Britain – defend free movement

ANDREW BURGIN

There are many aspects of life in Britain that those who voted leave hope will improve with Brexit. On holiday in Suffolk just after the June 23rd referendum (where 60% voted leave) my wife Kate and I were surprised to be told by the skipper on a coastal boat trip that Brussels was responsible for problems facing the avocet bird population on Orford Ness: in a fit of ecological correctness gone mad, the Eurocrats had apparently banned the culling of the local gull population, a competitor species that hails from foreign parts.

In fact, avocets were initially wiped out in Britain in the 19th century because we ate their eggs. Fortunately the avocet population had survived in other parts of Europe and they subsequently made their return to Orford. The truth is that EU funding underpins much of the nature conservation effort in the UK and its future is now uncertain. Yet the anti-EU, anti-immigrant narrative now intrudes everywhere, however baselessly, largely unchallenged.

Apart from supposedly protecting the local 'British' wildlife we are told that Brexit will mean ending the free movement of labour and controlling migration. This will lead to higher wages and increased employment among the native population and ease the shortage of housing and other social services. Moreover democracy will be restored – we will have our country back.

For the right, Brexit opens the door to freeing Britain from the stifling regulatory embrace of the European Union, allowing our national entrepreneurial spirit to once again reign free in the world at large; for some on the left, it is an essential first step on the path to a socialist Britain.

Those on the left who called for a Remain vote in the referendum, did so, not because we harboured illusions in the progressive nature of the EU, but because the Leave campaign was fuelled and dominated by reactionary politics. We believed that a Leave victory would empower the right rather than the left, and that far from providing a solution to any of the fundamental problems facing the working class it would open the way to further defeats. The post-Brexit treaties and legislative settlements would be seized upon by the government as a further opportunity for deregulation and attacks on our rights.

IMMIGRATION AND REFUGEES

The most reactionary feature of the campaign – and the most effective notwithstanding its dishonesty – was the way that all the ills of British society were laid at the door of immigration. Endless newspaper front pages told us how damaging and harmful immigrants and refugees were to the British way of life – this was the underlying message of the Leave campaign.

The fact that government policies are to blame for the shortages and cuts ascribed to migrants was disregarded, and the real economic benefits brought to our society and economy as a result of migration were airbrushed out of the referendum debate. So it is that the belief that curbing immigration will have a beneficial effect on British society has gained widespread currency and this belief was the driving force behind the Leave campaign.

Even among those who supported Remain and across a broad swathe of the labour movement the view that the free movement of people is detrimental to the interests of the British working class has taken hold.

A few days before the referendum vote the leader of Unite, the largest private sector union in Britain, made his views clear. Len McCluskey, writing in *The Guardian,* said he was not surprised that Labour voters were concerned about immigration: 'In the last 10 years, there has been a gigantic experiment at the expense of ordinary workers. Countries with vast historical differences in wage rates and living standards have been brought together in a common labour market ... The result has been sustained pressure on living standards, a systematic attempt to hold down wages and to cut the costs of social provision for working people'.

Following the referendum McCluskey has written further on this question arguing that 'workers have always done best when the labour supply is restricted and communities are stable'.

Leading figures from Labour's front bench team such as Andy Burnham and Clive Lewis have weighed into this debate detailing what they see as the many problems that free movement brings. Burnham, further exploring the stable communities theme, has argued that 'our reluctance in confronting this [free movement] debate is undermining the cohesion of our communities and the safety of our streets'.

The view that immigration and particularly free movement within the European Union has been responsible for lowering wages, diminishing social services and creating unemployment is widely held. But is this actually the case? And will Brexit create the conditions for raising the wages and employment levels of 'native' British workers?

The evidence suggests not. The argument that EU migration is responsible for a reduction in wage levels is tendentious to say the least. The enlargement of the EU in 2004, when 75 million people joined, did not lead to a downward pressure on wages. That took place after the crash of 2008. It is *since* the recession – which began with the credit crunch and the bailing out of the banks that led to the longest and deepest slump in a century – that we have seen substantial pay cuts. Allowing for inflation, average wages fell by 8 to 10 percent in the six years after the global financial crisis of 2008. Yet commentators generally don't mention the great crash in their analysis, so we are left with the impression that immigration is the source of these wage cuts – whereas the reality is that wages overall rose during the period 2004-8 when there was significant large-scale EU migration.

Most studies and reports show that immigration is a net contributor to the economy overall and, as far as average wages are concerned, it has a marginal impact and may actually lead to a small increase in average wages. Where there is an impact on wages – and it is a small one – it is on low wages, and its impact is felt primarily by existing migrant workers and not by UK-born workers. Moreover, the first systematic study of the effect of large-scale EU migration on the employment of UK-born workers showed no overall effect. Although some studies (Migrant Advisory Service) show that non-EU migration was associated with a reduction in the employment of UK-born workers over the period 1995-2010, there were no statistically significant effects for EU immigration.

In fact nearly all studies of the effect of migration on jobs and wages neglect to include the effect of job creation through enterprise by migrants. Migrants create more jobs than their actual numbers.

Recent research on the impact of Brexit by the National Institute of Economic and Social Research (NIESR) suggests that the effect of restrictions on migration will be almost as damaging as restrictions on trade. The negative effects – cutting growth of GDP by between 3.4% and 5.4% over a decade – would far outweigh any modest effect on the wages of workers in low-skilled jobs. One of the report's authors said: 'Prior to the referendum, a number of analyses estimated the long-term impacts of Brexit on the UK economy; but none incorporated the impacts of Brexit-induced reductions in migration. Our estimates suggest that the negative impacts on per-capita GDP will be significant, potentially approaching those from reduced trade.' The NIESR research shows that ending free movement would possibly increase unskilled wages by 0.1% over a five-year period and probably not even that, given the deleterious effects of ending free movement on the economy as a whole.

Whether the ending of free movement would itself reduce immigration is a moot point. In Lincolnshire and other agricultural areas there was a significant Leave vote, yet already farmers, many of whom themselves voted Leave, who rely largely on labour from Eastern Europe to pick their crops, are calling for work schemes to allow those migrants to work here on a temporary basis. So those workers would see their rights of permanent residence removed and would be reduced to the status of more exploitable casual workers. Ending free movement would therefore mean a return to sector-based schemes for foreign workers. This would restrict the rights of EU workers to temporary stays with no rights for family members. And because workers on those schemes are not included in immigration figures the benefit to the government would be to be able to show a decrease in the immigration figures whilst the employers still had access to labour. But for working class communities such schemes are liable to increase the instability that McCluskey talks about. There will be little incentive for temporary migrant workers to integrate into local communities.

As far as unemployment is concerned, the NIESR research also shows that immigration to Britain has little or no impact on overall levels of unemployment, even when the economy is in recession. There appears to be no link between migrant inflows and the overall level of those claiming jobseeker's allowance. This is almost certainly a reflection of the fact that most migrants are filling jobs for which local labour is not available. EU free movement is therefore not only a positive for the host country but it is an advance for the European working class as a whole. Rather than being 'guest' workers with few rights, those who work in other EU countries have rights and protections as EU citizens. These rights need to be extended rather than re-treated from.

WORKING CLASS SUPPORT FOR BREXIT

Clearly attitudes towards immigration are not entirely shaped by lived experience. In many areas with low migration such as Wales and the North East, large sections of the working class voted Leave. This serves to underline the fact that working class support for Brexit was driven primarily by economic instability – poor housing, low wages, job insecurity in areas experiencing severe social and economic deprivation – combined with the misperception that immigrants are to blame for these problems rather than government policies. Unemployment and demoralisation, together with a decline in trade union organisation in those areas, also fed an anti-immigrant narrative which has been driven by the media and by the emergence and development of UKIP.

The reality is that reducing immigration and ending free movement of labour is most likely to result in a fall in overall living standards and would actually lead to a downward pressure on wages and an increase in unemployment. A Brexit Britain driven by the free market policies of the current Tory government will not improve the lives of those working class Leave voters but will make them worse.

We should avoid extending our opposition to the existing structures and policies of the EU – notably its neo-liberal cuts, austerity and privatisation agenda – to the absolutely essential engagement with the working class, politically and economically, at a pan-European level. The dominant slogans of the Leave campaign – 'take back control' and 'we want our country back' with their subtexts of insularity and nationalism and implied hostility to the workers of other European countries – are illusory and reactionary. So too are the politics of those on the left who see an exit from the EU on the terms of the right as something progressive in itself.

A WAVE OF RACISM

The Leave campaign was built on a wave of racism and xenophobia, a British pro-Remain MP was murdered by a far right activist, and no lie was too outrageous to be believed: that Brexit would mean £350 million freed up each week for the NHS, that a Remain outcome would mean 70 million Turkish people coming to live here and claim benefits.

Following the vote the promises on the NHS were quickly withdrawn, but the anti-immigrant lies had whipped up such an atmosphere of permissive hostility that this rapidly led to a dramatic increase in racist and xenophobic attacks. A Polish man was murdered and his friend badly beaten by a group of teenagers in Essex for the 'crime' of speaking to each other in Polish.

Some on the left who supported the Leave campaign tended to play down the racist upsurge – but this increase in hate crime was an entirely predictable response to the vile campaign that had preceded it. The Leave vote emboldened the racists.

In fact, the referendum outcome further fuelled already existing anti-Muslim bigotry with increasing reports of women being assaulted and having their hijabs torn off. What took place was a dovetailing of all the bogus concerns around immigration with the reactionary campaign against Muslims and refugees on the basis of the perceived impossibility of their integration into British society.

The wrong position of some on the left regarding the upsurge in racism stemmed from their misperception of the Leave outcome as an advance for the left and the working class – not least their failure to recognise that the millions of European migrant workers living in Britain are part of the British and the European working class. They were denied a vote in the referendum even though they have been living and working here for many years and in some cases decades.

This narrow national approach contributes to racism and will only divide the working class. Further to that, claims had been made during the campaign that a Brexit vote would strengthen the Corbyn leadership and hugely weaken the Conservative Party. In fact, following the vote the Tory government united under a new, more right-wing leadership and was strengthened. Within the Labour Party, the Corbyn leadership came under massive and sustained attack from the party's right, now given its long-awaited excuse to try to unseat Corbyn based on his perceived lack of commitment to a Remain victory. This was precisely the opposite outcome to that predicted by those on the left who supported Leave, some of whom had argued that the Tory government would probably fall and that if a Conservative government survived, it would be hopelessly fragile.

The May government is not 'hopelessly fragile'. The Tories closed ranks to unite in the interests of their party and class and, given a positive boost by May's clever presentation of her non-Eton background and longstanding ministerial experience, they remain well ahead in the polls. An early general election is unlikely given the current fixed term regulation and the fact that the government has a workable overall majority. But the government does have serious problems about how to deal with Brexit and there are serious divisions in the ruling class. This is uncharted territory – apparently there are insufficient experts to actually deal with the technical challenges of the necessary legislation – and it is also extremely unpopular with a large minority of the population.

The politics of Brexit will dominate British political discourse for the foreseeable future. It is essential that the Labour Party, which is twisting in the wind over the question of free movement, manages to project a clear vision of the socialist Europe we need to work towards and does not fall into the trap of seeking illusory opportunities for Brexit Britain.

PRO-EUROPE PROTESTS

The days and weeks following the referendum were notable for a wave of mass pro-Europe protests, to the extent that one could say that a new movement is emerging to challenge Brexit. More than 4 million people signed a petition demanding a second referendum within days of the vote. So far given the poor response from the Labour Party this new anti-Brexit movement has been dominated by the Liberal Democrats. The strategy of the centre-right is to attempt to overturn the referendum decision in a second vote, in a futile attempt to maintain British EU membership as it was before the first.

Such an approach can only have negative consequences. Not only has that ship sailed but such a campaign would only fuel the right in this country. Already there are those like Aaron Banks, UKIP's main financier, who are preparing to launch a new super-charged UKIP in the event that there is a serious attempt to overturn the Brexit result. In this context we need to engage with this anti-Brexit movement on a positive pro-European basis, but clearly arguing for a re-founded union, a different type of Europe which seeks to preserve the progressive elements of EU membership but to go well beyond them in terms of democratic, political and economic reform.

The terms of Brexit are now the key site of struggle for the left and progressive forces in Britain. There is no doubt that they will be highly contested. The Brexiteers charged with overseeing the process, Boris Johnson, David Davies and Liam Fox, will try to dilute or remove those trade union and social rights which have been underwritten by the EU. The Human Rights Act will be scrapped. Our job is to strenuously resist that.

There are those on the left who are calling for us to 're-spect' the referendum result. We do not 'respect' the result as there was a real democratic deficit in the referendum because of the lies and racism that drove the Leave campaign. It is more accurate to say that we 'accept' the referendum outcome in the same way that we accept the result of an election.

Accepting the outcome doesn't mean ceasing to fight at every level, in the same way that when the Tories win an election we struggle against their reactionary policies at every step, fighting to defeat them electorally, and mounting campaigns in our communities to fight for our rights and defend and extend what we have already won. We will have to fight every step of the way to prevent the Brexit treaties and parliamentary legislation being a deregulatory jamboree in the interests of the ruling class.

We need to campaign actively against little Brexit Britain and the stripping away of our rights, and chief among those campaigns must be to defend the right to free movement. Free movement is an enormous step forward for the European working class, allowing the possibility of the creation of pan-European spheres of struggle. It recognises the essential fact that the integration of Europe politically and economically is a vital step forward for the working class internationally. The struggle is not to undermine the gain that free movement represents – some left Leave supporters refer to it as 'so-called' freedom of movement – but to recognise its importance and to fight to defend it and extend it.

Not only free movement but migration in general must be defended; it is historically a powerful source of progressive development and we fight for open borders and for European integration. We oppose fortress Europe but we understand that the ending of free movement in Europe will make extending that right to all more – not less – difficult. We also recognise that the European integration that we need is not possible within the capitalist framework represented by the European Union.

PAN-EUROPEAN MOVEMENT

So the task is not to agitate for a second referendum or to ignore the Brexit vote but it is to recognise that a pan-European movement is necessary to create the democratic and federal Europe that can begin to solve the problems that the working class faces internationally. This cannot be achieved within a national framework.

The most powerful moments in recent working class struggle in Europe have been those which have reached beyond national borders. The British miners' strike in the 1980s and the French strikes of the 1990s and the mass recent struggles of the Greek working class have all found deep reserves of support from across the continent. Free movement represents the concretisation of the European working class and its ending would be a reactionary step, bringing no economic benefit to the so-called native working classes of each country and politically weakening all working class forces across Europe.

The struggle over Brexit is the most important political challenge that we face. The consequences of unmitigated Tory exit terms are too terrible to contemplate, so there is much work to be done. But this is also an opportunity to campaign and argue for an alternative, for the socialist Europe that we wish to see. Writing that in Britain may sound hopelessly utopian, but this is actually a vision shared by millions across Europe, many of them already organised in unions, parties and movements advancing those arguments. And this is also an opportunity to engage with the many hundreds of thousands of young people in this country who voted to remain – not because they sought to defend the neo-liberal institutions of the EU but because they instinctively grasped the importance of going beyond our national borders, feeling a real allegiance to a social Europe.

These are complex issues that cannot be settled in a single-question referendum. Referenda are in any case of questionable democratic value and are notoriously the province of the dictator. But neither can these issues be solved on a national basis. The 'take back control' message of the Leave campaign claimed that they could, but that was a reactionary illusion based on little Englander nationalism. It also had the effect of exculpating our own ruling class and institutions for their undemocratic and austerity driven agendas by blaming Brussels, when the attacks on the working class will be even more brutal following Brexit.

So the British framework is clearly inadequate for the advances we need to make. An essential first step in this direction is an open discussion on all the issues that form the fabric of people's everyday lives throughout Europe – on jobs, austerity, social services and wages. Such a debate and struggle across Europe has the possibility of affirming a shared belonging to Europe and the consolidation of collective struggle and strategic coordination to achieve the victories that are necessary to secure the basic existence of so many people's lives.

There are now calls for referenda to be held across Europe. These calls are coming primarily from the far right – Marine Le Pen in France, Geert Wilders in Holland and from Italy and Sweden. There are some on the left echoing these demands, believing that the left will be the main beneficiary of the breakup of the EU, but this is illusory. The far right sees itself as the beneficiary of these developments. Thus Marine Le Pen called the Brexit vote the 'most important moment since the fall of the Berlin wall', and Donald Trump termed his recent victory in the US presidential election 'Brexit plus plus plus'. The Brexit result *was* of enormous significance but not in the way those on the left who voted leave believe. Both the vote for Brexit and the election of the right-wing demagogue Donald Trump are part of a dangerous turn to the right internationally.

We need to reject specious arguments on free movement and migration. A movement based on opposition to Brexit and defence of migration must be built up, uniting all those under threat from the turn to the right – migrant workers and refugees with all those who face continued austerity.

A broad campaign is needed irrespective of whether people voted Remain or Leave, without giving ground to the idea that the Brexit vote was either progressive or an opportunity for the left. Racism and xenophobia have been legitimised by both Brexit and Trump and they herald a new reactionary period in world politics. This poses a challenge for the European left as a whole.

We have to campaign for a refounded European union on a democratic and anti-capitalist basis. The first slogan in this campaign must be 'Defend Free Movement'.

Andrew Burgin is a national officer of Left Unity, Britain's radical left party.

Europe's problem with nationalism

LUKE COOPER

Britain's vote to leave the European Union (EU) is the big-gest electoral calamity to have befallen the left since Margaret Thatcher's election in 1979. Parallels can often be drawn too hastily, but the dangers of the current moment are every bit as serious as the rise of Thatcher's anti-trade union, individualist and free market-driven populism was for socialists in the late 1970s. Stuart Hall famously coined the term 'Thatcherism' in a perceptive commentary he penned in 1979, which warned the left not to underestimate the ideological and cultural potential of Thatcher's worldview.[1] Hall's prediction proved prophetic. Thatcherism's marriage of free market liberalism with authori-tarian nationalism would go on to shape the assumptions of the British political landscape for the next four decades. Indeed, it is impossible to understand why the majority of the British electorate opted to leave the EU without situating the vote in a longer trajectory of developments that began with Thatcher.

What the result represents above all else is the triumph of the most populist elements of Thatcher's ideology over those more pragmatic components that sought to carefully steward British society so as to ensure the interests of big capital. Restructuring British capitalism to shift the balance of power away from organ-ised labour, and undertaking an accompanying financialization that allowed capital to diversify and globalise its reach, may have involved significant class conflicts and instability.[2] But such battles were undertaken for a clear purpose in the 1980s: to create a more market-driven capitalist economy. Authoritarianism and nationalism – encapsulated by the quasi police state that confronted the miners at the Battle of Orgreave and the jingoism of the Falklands War, respectively – were vital components of delivering this new deal for capital. When the miners were declared the 'enemy within' they were essentially cast as an anti-British conspiracy against a project of national salvation. The draconian 'law and order' state[3] that fostered riots in Brixton and Tottenham similarly cultivated a sense of populist fear towards the marginalised and oppressed undoubtedly useful to cohere the populace around Thatcher's economic programme. But her nationalism was perhaps most visibly expressed in the infamous 'Bruges speech' where she offered an emphatic rejection of European political union:

> 'We have not successfully rolled back the frontiers of the state in Britain, only to see them re-imposed at a European level with a European super-state exercising a new dominance from Brussels'.[4]

This position created a powerful legacy within the Conservative Party. Eurosceptic Thatcherites over the next three decades would dedicate themselves to opposing what they saw as a conspiracy to build a super-state that extinguished British sovereignty.

BRITAIN'S EXIT: THATCHER'S NATIONALIST LEGACY

In the 1980s, however, Thatcherism's organic nationalism provided an essential point of cohesion to a class project that was a perfectly logical response by the ruling classes to a long period of economic crisis. Fast-forward to today and one can see how the legacy of Bruges was to spawn an altogether more ideological form of populism within Tory ranks. The Leave campaign in Britain's EU referendum exemplified the rise of a form of right-wing populism in Europe that often appears to abhor pragmatic compromise. It cannot be argued in the same way that it constitutes a logical response of capital to Britain's economic difficulties. If there is specificity to the variant of Thatcherite populism articulated so successfully by Patel, Johnson, Farage, Leadsom, and Gove in the referendum campaign, then surely it lies in a desire to put *nation above class;* an ethos encapsulated by the 'take back control' slogan. Implicitly, and sometimes explicitly,[5] this approach draws heavily on Britain's imperial tradition, looking back to the colonial era as a time of sovereign independence. In doing so, they promoted the myth that sovereignty was absolute; it could either be present or absent with no ambiguities in between allowed for. Only in the context of Britain's colonial history and its one-time hegemony could such claims have rhetorical force.[6]

Since the 1980s financial liberalisation has, of course, had constraining implications on the policy choices of governments. In this sense, a key contextual difference between the rise of Thatcherism and contemporary right-wing populism can be summarised thus: whereas the former made up part of the genesis of free market (or 'neoliberal') globalisation, the latter has emerged in the context of a crisis of this economic order. In much of Europe right-wing populism has therefore been an explicit reaction to globalism. But in its British variant – unlike Marine Le Pen's Front National, for instance – nationalist populism remains 'globalist', rather than protectionist, in its desired economic orientation. It promotes a vision of Britain as a light-touch regulation, low tax, free market economy tied into global markets but engaging in aggressive neoliberal restructuring to attract inward investment. Far from assuring the British electorate's 'right to rule' – i.e. its sovereignty over its own affairs – the deepening of neoliberal globalisation this entails would make policy decisions even more circumscribed by global markets. But however attractive, in the abstract, this might be to sections of big capital, the latter's primary concern with long-term investment security and access to Europe's single market meant that Vote Leave won scant support from the corporate economic elite. Unlike in Thatcher's case, therefore, big capital remained un-persuaded of the viability of the Leave campaign agenda.

Herein, however, lies part of the appeal and ultimate success of the Leave movement. At a time when millions have experienced stagnating or falling living standards, the official campaign to remain in the EU was burdened by an establishment and corporate feel throughout. It sent a clear message that if you wanted to make a protest vote against the establishment, then voting Leave was the way to go. The Leave campaign's populism combined aversion to reasoned argument, a preparedness to consciously mislead the public as well as the making of sweeping promises of change. The British net contribution to the EU budget was deliberately, and quite infamously, overstated with extra revenues promised for the cash-starved NHS. Michael Gove – someone who one could reasonably describe as a member of the establishment *par excellence* – appealed directly to working class voters, attacking the 'job destroying' EU run by 'sneering elites'.[7] He would later have to apologise for comparing economic experts warning of the dangers of Brexit to 'Nazis'.[8] Architect of the Vote Leave campaign, Dominic Cummings, who previously cut his teeth in the anti-euro movement of the early 2000s,[9] coined the term 'take back control' as part of a strategy of deliberately exaggerated messaging. The emotive language cut against the technocratic warnings of the official Remain camp, but was, in true populist fashion, also designed to win support from across the left-right spectrum. Who, after all, is against being 'in control'? Only occasionally did the mask slip from this populist appeal to the interests of the working Briton. Priti Patel went off message by calling for the slashing of EU social and employment protections in post-Brexit Britain,[10] but generally the Leave campaign stuck faithfully to the Cummings line.

Vote Leave originally intended to primarily focus on these arguments. In April, a Channel 4 journalist, no doubt having been briefed by campaign insiders, described their 'squeamishness' on immigration and their desire to leave the more openly xenophobic arguments to Nigel Farage and Leave.EU. He even stated that Michael Gove had 'never been comfortable with the Theresa May line on immigration' and 'was one of the most consistent and outspoken voices against hardline immigration controls'.[11] Such claims are obviously of questionable journalistic merit, especially considering the overtly anti-immigrant propaganda Vote Leave had already commissioned on EU expansion,[12] but they did nonetheless reflect a sensibility in the campaign that it had to avoid appearing to be too extreme. As opinion polls, however, showed that Leave was lagging behind Remain, and also demonstrated that immigration was the strongest card the campaign had to play,[13] Vote Leave soon 'discovered' their xenophobia.

Just eleven days later, the supposedly pro-immigration Gove wrote a shameful piece for the *Daily Mail*. Full of 'dog-whistle' racism from start to finish, the article heavily insinuated, in a manner only marginally more subtle than Donald Trump, that Albanians were all criminals and that the Balkan country only wished to join the EU to receive handouts from the British taxpayer.[14] Once it became bedded in as a strategy, playing the 'immigration card' worked. Of the 52 polls undertaken after Gove published his piece, Leave had a lead in 28 of them (54 per cent). In April and March the situation was reversed with Leave leading in just 15 of 37 polls (only 41 per cent).[15] A clever triangulation of nominally progressive discourses focusing on democracy and the NHS with nasty dog-whistle racism clearly won it for Leave. Indeed, this went further than playing the immigration card, but really played a 'race card', with scaremongering about non-white immigration from the predominantly Muslim countries of Albania and Turkey providing a modern day echo of Enoch Powell's infamous 'rivers of blood' speech.

It should really go without saying that the victory of such a campaign represented a major blow to the progressive left. Overwhelmingly, the most progressive sections of British society backed a Remain vote, many of them motivated not by illusions in the European institutions, but a keen sense of the nationalism and racism that was propelling the Leave campaign. Of course, the Leave vote did reflect significant levels of discontent and alienation in many working class communities. But this desire to protest electorally was activated by the right around a nationalist, and often racist, set of messages and demands. As Neil Faulkner explains:

> 'The real issue is this. The discontent at the base of society has been organised and mobilised by the Right, not the Left, and the whole of British politics has, in consequence, been shifted sharply to the right. Racism has become mainstream, legitimised in a way that has not been the case since at least the 1960s. This, furthermore, is a global phenomenon. The Brexit campaign was the local franchise of a worldwide syndicate that includes Donald Trump, Marine Le Pen, and Viktor Orban'.[16]

Indeed. Whether one points to the ascent of Donald Trump in the United States or the landslide victory of Narendra Modi in India, the twenty-first century rise of nationalist populism is a far from exclusively European problem. However, the strength of such far-right forces within Europe is especially troubling given the existence of a nominally strong framework for cooperation and project for political union: the EU. The rise of nationalism within such a transnational political project obviously indicates a deep crisis, one requiring explanation and critical reflection. Two factors have conjoined to create this crisis: widespread economic discontent produced by a failed economic model, on the one hand, and Europe's long-term problem with nationalism, on the other. This toxic combination triggered the wave of right-wing populism. Ironically, the modus operandi of the EU reflects the 'incompleteness' of Europe's break with nationalism, not its success in creating a transnational union. The decision-making structures of the Eurozone area, for example, epitomise the kind of horse-trading typical of diplomatic manoeuvring amongst competing nation states. These divisions are further accentuated by the way in which neoliberal economic assumptions were institutionalised to impose a straitjacket on states in the Eurozone area. Cooperation is the loser in a system that has come to resemble a 'zero sum game'. Nationalist populism has been the key beneficiary of these political conditions.

Confusing the rise of anti-European nationalism with a progressive rupture in the neoliberal order has led some on the left to argue that we should ride, and not confront, the new populism. Stathis Kouvelakis, for example, has condemned the left's reluctance to invoke the language of nationhood, arguing that 'if we start from the premise any positive reference to the nation inherently produces nationalism, racism, imperial and colonial nostalgia, then the Left is doomed to lose this political battle by losing touch with the working and the popular classes.'[17] Such a comment is riddled with assumptions regarding one's understanding of the modern working class subject and its supposed preference for nationalist solutions. But even if one accepts that the working class as a whole is as mired in nationalism as Kouvelakis imagines it is surely something to be confronted creatively, rather than accepted as inevitable. In the British context it appears above all else to be primarily a crisis of English identity – and even then one subject to a high level of geographical determination. Rethinking the multi-layered constitutional relationship between the communities of the United Kingdom and Europe could help offset this, perhaps through an English parliament as part of an equal federal settlement with the other home nations.

But it is simply wrong to believe a 'good' anti-European nationalism can be constructed as an alternative to the 'bad', i.e. racist and xenophobic, anti-Europeanism on display in the referendum. Such a view ignores the geopolitical and economic reality within which this apparent 'choice' over how the national community is imagined takes place. In the context of a crisis-ridden European system that largely retains open borders internally the very likely effect of striking an implicit united front with nationalists against European integration would be the restoration of borders all over Europe.[18] However much one might attempt to construct an anti-racist and progressive sense of British-ness, the *othering* qualities of nationalism – the construction of the alien 'them' so important to the unity of 'us' – cannot be dispensed with.[19] The call for the British to 'take back control' was, and *is*, a call for the non-British, including the many migrant workers resident within the polity, to have *less control.* In other words, the logic of nationalism will always assert itself against such seemingly clever attempts at triangulation in a manner that very obviously imperils an internationalist left politics.

ANARCHIC EUROPE IN THE POST-CRISIS WORLD

A vital part of any anti-capitalist project must involve transcending this system of national conflict so as to address the truly global issues, such as climate change or economic failure, that do not recognise national boundaries. Only a left with a truly global horizon can answer this exigency to rethink the conventional (national) level on which we imagine political change to be possible. In itself, this is a far from novel idea. For as long as there has been a critical understanding of globalisation-from-above as a top down process of neoliberal reordering, there has been a discussion of how to shape an alternative globalisation-from-below. Looking back on some of these early commentaries in historical retrospect one is struck by how, in spite of the huge social changes seen over the last two decades, the core *problématique* concerning the material ability of the forces of neoliberal globalisation to significantly narrow the policy options available to national states remains as true as ever. As Richard Falk suggested back in 1997, the financial liberalisation of the preceding decades increased capital mobility, making a capital-friendly policy essential to avoid capital flight:

'The negative essence of this dynamic, as unfolding within the present historical timeframe, is to impose on governments the discipline of global capital in a manner that promotes economistic policy making in national arenas of decision, subjugating the outlook of governments, political parties, leaders and elites and often accentuating distress to vulnerable and disadvantaged regions and peoples... This set of circumstances, if not properly modified, presages a generally grim future for human society, including a tendency to make alternative orientations towards economic policy appear irrelevant; to the extent believed, this induces a climate of resignation and despair'.[20]

This 'climate of resignation and despair' was more than evident in the EU referendum, particularly in post-industrial and rural areas outside the large metropolitan cities.[21] Some of the most remarkable polling undertaken in the referendum demonstrated the total lack of trust Leave voters had in virtually every component of public-facing civil society: not only politicians, academics and journalists, but also sportspeople, actors, and entertainers.[22] Another poll showed that 46 per cent of Leave voters believed the ballot would be rigged.[23] These are cultural signifiers of a dramatic breakdown of faith in the political process. It arises out of the way that decades of neoliberalism have combined material pressures and legitimising narratives to narrow policy choices, sucking the ideological life out of politics.[24]

For the global justice movement of the early 2000s raising the banner of an alternative globalisation-from-below made sense, in part because the limits of political action within the confines of national societies were acutely recognised. Despite all the technological and social change the world has seen in the last two decades, many of the central problems of the globalisation epoch for the left remain relatively unchanged. How, in particular, does a geographically diffuse and heterogeneous global working class challenge a capitalist system whose strength lies in its ability to combine capital mobility with a robust set of international institutions that operate on a basis historically structured by free market liberalisation? A retreat into economically closed societies, re-running the political experiments that failed so abysmally in the last century, might appear tempting in these conditions, but such a move offers neither a means to raise the living standards of the working classes in a significant and lasting way, nor an answer to the global problems of our age. From the need for an environmentally sustainable economy to clamping down on tax avoidance, or tackling the global hunger crisis, there are no simple, national solutions.

In its broad contours, these fundamental questions of strategy have remained the central ones for the left as neoliberalism has shown a remarkable capacity to grow even stronger, and more embedded, with each crisis. If, with David Harvey,[25] one sees neoliberalism as a project of class power, intent on the permanent erosion of barriers, real or imagined,[26] to the profitability and growth of capital, then even the mere hope, which many entertained,[27] that the crisis of 2008 would lead to a break with this framework appears rather naïve. Neoliberalism sought to transform the state into a regulatory vehicle primarily concerned with the growth of private wealth, and not the delivery of public goods. Complex and inefficient command bureaucracies, such as those established in British higher education, or on the railways, neither of which bore any resemblance to a 'free market' properly understood, were created in order to open up sectors previously run on the basis of public need to competition and private investment. Looked at in these terms the pragmatic defence of financial interests since the crisis of 2008 is consistent with the longer history of neoliberalism.

Within Europe the particular physiognomy of the crisis, however, has been shaped by the EU's unique status, in contrast to other regional economic blocs, as not only a free trade area, but also an attempt to move towards political union. To say that it has failed to live up to the grand statements made around the time of its launch would be quite an understatement. Jacques Chirac typified this outlook but his remarks now look rather ill fated in the context of years of deepening economic crisis:

> 'The euro is a victory for Europe. After a century of being torn apart, of wars and tribulations, our continent is finally affirming its identity and power in peace, unity and stability'.[28]

Perhaps even more tragic were the remarks of Costas Simitis, the Greek Prime Minister, on the country's entry into the Eurozone in 2001, who spoke optimistically of 'greater stability' and the 'opening up of new horizons'.[29] As the Greek people have experienced, this new horizon of Eurozone membership came at a hugely *destabilising* and impoverishing cost with the economy contracting by an eye-watering 25 per cent since the financial crisis of 2008.[30] But Greece is only the most extreme example of how the global slump has affected many Eurozone countries. While in each case there are, of course, national peculiarities, states as diverse as France and Portugal share the common problem that they cannot compete successfully with German exports on the level playing field necessitated by a single currency area. For the southern European economies, in particular, the misleading appearance of monetary stability in the 2000s also fuelled the easy money credit boom, as capital flowed in from German and French banks – only to then flow out rapidly as the squeeze in lending after the financial crisis left these states bankrupt. Locked in conditions of monetary union they do not have the ability to devalue their currency, which under-competitive states would normally use to cheapen exports. This puts the onus of devaluing wages and prices to boost growth wholly on the austere economic measures we have seen since 2008 – with brutal consequences for the people. 'Normal' single currency areas, i.e. usually nation-states, will offset this problem by having mechanisms for fiscal transfer that kick in when a region is affected by a downturn. When states in America enter recession, for example, they will pay less into the federal budget, but due to the existence of a nationwide social security system they will receive extra fiscal transfers into their economy as unemployment rises. The sharing of risks this entails is seen as one of the benefits of a common currency area, but simply does not exist in Europe.[31]

These problems have not come 'out of the blue', but were anticipated by critics of the Maastricht protocols *at the time* of their creation in the early 1990s. A young Ed Balls, who famously advised Gordon Brown during the period he successfully kyboshed Tony Blair's euro ambitions, was one of many observers to lay out these problems in a succinctly written Fabian Society pamphlet published in 1992.[32] Typically, underpinning this failure to establish a sustainable single currency framework were geopolitical considerations, i.e. the assertion of *national* interests over collective ones. The European Exchange Rate Mechanism (ERM), the forerunner to the euro in which participant currencies were pegged to the value of the Deutschmark, placed significant power in the hands of the German Bundesbank to effectively determine the economic fate of participant countries. In exchange for giving up this power the German government insisted on the now infamous 'convergence criteria', which placed an even harsher straitjacket on economic policy for members than that which they already faced through disciplining logic of liberalised capital markets *per se*. Perry An-

derson rather presciently anticipated at the time that these fiscal measures would lead to an extreme form of neoliberalism:

'What is the social logic of the monetary union scheduled
to come into force by the end of the decade? In a system
of the kind envisaged at Maastricht, national macro-eco-
nomic policy becomes a thing of the past: all that remains
to member-states are distributive options on – necessarily reduced – expenditures within balanced budgets, at
competitive levels of taxation. The historic commitments
of both Social and Christian Democracy to full employment and social services of the traditional welfare state,
already scaled down or cut back, would cease to have
any further institutional purchase. This is a revolutionary
prospect. The single obligation of the projected European
Central Bank, more restrictive even than the charter of
the Federal Reserve, is the maintenance of price stability. The protective and regulative functions of existing
national states will be dismantled, leaving sound money
as the sole regulator, as in the classical liberal model of
the epoch before Keynes. The new element – namely, the
supranational character of the future monetary authority – would serve to reinforce such a historical reversion:
elevated higher above national electorates than its predecessors, it will be more immune, and not only by statute,
from popular pressures. Put simply, a federal Europe in
this sense would not mean – as Conservatives in Britain
fear – a super-state, but *less* state'.[33]

During the Eurozone crisis these rules have been dogmati-
cally enforced as the conditions attached to debt relief have imposed severe cutbacks in spending coupled with aggressive free
market restructuring of labour laws and tax systems in a seemingly futile attempt to meet convergence requirements. While
designed to encourage investment, in most states, especially

Greece, they have had the opposite effect as a vicious cycle of austerity leading to slackening demand, requiring, in turn, more austerity to meet Eurozone rules, has blunted economic growth. With no fiscal mechanisms – such as common taxation and social security systems – to even out economic development within the Eurozone area, the divide between northern and peripheral spheres has grown stark. For while prior to the crisis, the Eurozone economies were broadly growing in tandem, since then they have diverged rapidly, making it even harder for a single monetary policy to meet the needs of all the participant countries.[34] In other words, Europe has managed to create a common monetary system with no redistributive mechanisms between states, accentuating economic unevenness between wealthier and poorer regions, and combining all the worst facets of a central banking system – the exclusive focus on price stability at the expense of growth – with none of the advantages of exchange rate flexibility.

At the root of these failings is the highly peculiar contemporary form the nation-state system has assumed in Europe. Political scientists who study such relations between states often utilise the concept of 'anarchy' to refer, not to the libertarian ideology, but an inter-state system made up of many competing political entities without a single superordinate authority with power over them. Because of the partial and incomplete steps that have been taken to political union, Europe has a *sui generis* ('of a special type') form of anarchic system. In this hybrid version, the institutional framework for EU member states is shaped by the accumulated decisions of the multilateral treaties over time, which have created a technocratic quasi executive in the form of the Commission, but one that is still largely subordinated to the bartering process seen in the intergovernmental meetings. Inter-state decision-making in which each nation is *formally* equal still tends to predominate, with only the relatively weak European Parliament providing a direct democratic link between the peoples of Europe and its supranational institutions.

It was also the meetings of the Eurogroup, which is, in principle, merely an informal meeting of the governments in the single currency area, which doomed Greece to its fate, and rightly led many observers to conclude Europe was suffering from a profound democratic deficit. But while the latter is very real, it is important to identify its source accurately, because it does not lie in the existence of a 'super-state' in the way that eurosceptics, on the left as well as the right, often imagine. There is nothing about an anarchic system that provides for a strong relationship to democracy. Because power is always distributed unevenly amongst the states that constitute the system, the materially stronger states are likely to dominate the weaker. The Eurogroup was no exception to this general rule as the balance of power within it reflects the strength of the German economy and the country's successful forging of alliances that cut across 'old' – the core, founding members – and 'new' Europe. Once added to the political hostility that mainstream parties had to the leftist posture of Syriza, and the growth of nationalistic sentiment in Europe's north that perversely viewed the bailouts as altruistic, then there was little scope for a compromise favourable to Greece. In other words, the Greek crisis is indicative of the failure of Europe to move towards a real political union with representative, democratic institutions and mechanisms for fiscal transfer between states. This failure has led to wealthier states enjoying the power to determine the fate of the weaker – a democratic deficit typical of anarchic systems.

Nationalism is growing across Europe as a result of these economic and geopolitical conditions. The long-term failure to create a European public space that might overcome the continent's national divisions has been made harder by the zero-sum-like economic environment we have seen since 2008. During the Greek negotiations in July 2015 the threat of the Finns Party, a junior coalition partner, to bring down the Finnish government if Greece was granted a bailout, signified Europe's breakdown of solidarity amidst rising nationalist sentiment.[35]

In this sense, the section of the left looking for a de facto rapprochement with nationalism has to ignore the role that national conflict has played as a central factor within the Eurozone crisis. By not creating sufficiently redistributive mechanisms between states when the Euro was established beggar-thy-neighbour policies were built into the architecture of this system of *sui generis* anarchy. Paradoxically, perhaps, amidst the deep crisis of the neoliberal centre, it has fallen to the radical left[36] to advance the sensible policies[37] that could create conditions for a stable growth strategy within Europe.

In short, it falls to the left to challenge Europe's *problem with nationalism*. Those on the left proposing a project of national 'democratisation' as an alternative to a pan-European agenda are guilty of promoting the fallacy of equating an anarchic system with a form of democratic empowerment. Greece shows all too clearly how strong states can impose policies on weaker ones and, as such, underlines the pressing need for a transnational leftism. Classical left critiques of nationalism also appear to be easily forgotten by those asserting that Europe's contemporary vicissitudes offer the opportunity for the construction of a supposedly progressive set of left nationalisms. Even when nationalism takes on a clearly anti-hegemonic form subjectively determined to tackle neoliberal institutions, it remains a mechanism capable of subordinating internal class antagonisms to a superficially equitable sense of 'national interest'.[38] The inevitably challenging but vitally necessary alternative to this resuscitation of a left nationalism is to construct a class-based transnational politics.

FIGHT FOR A BETTER EUROPE, DON'T BEAT A RETREAT

These problems and aspirations are not new. It is simply that the stakes have been raised much higher in the post-crisis world as society has become more polarised between left and right. Back in 2003, for example, Teivo Teivainen warned of the dangers of invoking a simplistic *anti*-globalisation, which had troubling connotations, stood in tension with internationalism, and would lead to making *mistaken alliances*:

> 'It would, however, be analytically faulty and politically unwise simply to define the movements as being against globalisation, if the term is understood as the increasing transgression of nation-state borders on a worldwide level. Many of them are, I would claim, looking for a different kind of globalisation, although some may prefer to use the older term 'internationalism'. From a democratic perspective, the problem in some anti-globalisation rhetoric is that one easily ends up with rather strange bedfellows. Professing anti-globalisation pure and simple is not very helpful in terms of making a distinction between regulating the cross-border movements of speculative capital and those of black immigrants'.[39]

Looked at in the context of the successful Leave campaign in the EU referendum these remarks are rather apposite. The financial liberalisation, which has increased cross-border mobility for big capital, increasing the leverage and power it has over democratic governments, was given unconditional support by the vast majority of Brexit campaigners. Even limited attempts by the EU to undertake financial reform have been opposed by British governments, including the right wing Tory eurosceptics that delivered the Leave vote. These same individuals, however, have insisted that closing Britain's borders with the EU is central to their terms of negotiation. While elsewhere the far right often pursues something close to a genuine *anti*-globalisation agenda – combining an aggressively protectionist economic strategy with swingeing attacks on migrants and ethnic minority communities – in Britain populism has a distinctly 'globalist' colouration. The new international movements advocating an offensive on neoliberal hegemony across borders, and opposing the shortcut of exit, consequently have a particular importance in the British context. The many left radicals who came around the Another Europe Is Possible[40] campaign in the EU referendum sought to combine a defence of British membership with arguing for radical reform and a break with the austerity union logic of the institutions. Despite the great disappointment of the referendum we must not give up on this vision of a different Europe. Indeed, whereas once there was a tendency of grassroots social movements to 'take Europe for granted',[41] i.e. utilise the environment created by transnational cooperation but not make it a focus of campaigning, the crisis that has befallen the EU since 2010 has led to it becoming a key focus of activity. With a plethora of new initiatives now emerging and working together in the spirit of 'one no, many yeses', these movements offer hope that the tide of reaction can be turned.

We should, in short, not give up on the struggle for 'another Europe'.

Luke Cooper is Senior Lecturer in Politics at Anglia Ruskin University.

NOTES

1. Stuart Hall, 'The Great Moving Right Show', *Marxism Today*, January 1979, 14–20.
2. David Harvey, *A Brief History of Neoliberalism*, new edition (Oxford: Oxford University Press, 2007).
3. Stuart Hall et al., *Policing the Crisis: Mugging, the State, and Law and Order*, 1978 edition (London: Macmillan, 1978).
4. Margaret Thatcher, Speech to the College of Europe ('The Bruges Speech'), 20 September 1988. Available online: http://www.margaretthatcher.org/document/107332 (accessed 24 August 2016).
5. For example, see the comments of UKIP's Paul Nuttall the day before the referendum, 'Forget Brussels – the UK should be doing business with the Commonwealth, says PAUL NUTTALL', *Daily Express*, 22 June 2016, http://www.express.co.uk/comment/expresscomment/682269/Brussels-UK-business-Commonwealth-PAUL-NUTTALL-Ukip-trade (accessed 24 August 2016). Or, in a piece of fine self parody, Conservative MP Heather Wheeler's tweeting of a 'British Empire' tally in the Rio Olympics medal table, see 'Conservative MP praises "British empire" for Rio 2016 medal tally', *Guardian*, 22 August 2016, http://www.theguardian.com/politics/2016/aug/22/conservative-mp-praises-british-empire-for-rio-2016-medal-tally (accessed 24 August 2016).
6. P. Gilroy, *Postcolonial Melancholia* (New York: Columbia University Press, 2008).
7. 'EU debate: Michael Gove condemns "job-destroying" elites and "racist" immigration rules as he appeals to Britons to back "Project Hope"', *The Telegraph*, 4 June 2016, http://www.telegraph.co.uk/news/2016/06/03/eu-debate-michael-gove-faces-biggest-test-of-campaign-as-he-take1/ (accessed 24 August 2016).
8. 'Michael Gove apologises for comparing economic experts warning against Brexit to Nazis', *Independent*, 22 June 2016, http://www.independent.co.uk/news/uk/politics/eu-referendum-brexit-live-michael-gove-economy-economic-experts-nazis-apology-a7095536.html (accessed 24 August 2016).
9. 'Combative Brexiter who took control of Vote Leave operation', *Financial Times*, 14 June 2016, http://www.ft.com/cms/s/2/cceb7038-30cc-11e6-bda0-04585c31b153.html#axzz4Hmms83VW (accessed 24 August 2016).
10. 'Who let the cats out? Priti Patel suggests we could lose half our EU work rights after #Brexit', Touchstone Blog, 18 May 2016, http://

touchstoneblog.org.uk/2016/05/let-cats-priti-patel-suggests-lose-half-eu-work-rights-brexit/ (accessed 24 August 2016).

11. 'Vote Leave's "squeamishness about pressing the immigration button"', Channel 4 News Blog, Tuesday 19 April 2016, http://blogs.channel4.com/gary-gibbon-on-politics/vote-leaves-squeamishness-pressing-immigration-button/32664 (accessed 24 August 2016).

12. 'Vote Leave: "Party" Political Broadcast, 2016 UK in EU referendum', YouTube, https://www.youtube.com/watch?v=h_MzHFiu-6Y (accessed 24 August 2016).

13. 'Remain pulls ahead of Leave in EU referendum poll as David Cameron's leaflet hits home', *The Telegraph*, 19 April 2016, http://www.telegraph.co.uk/news/2016/04/18/remain-pulls-ahead-of-leave-in-eu-referendum-poll-as-david-camer/ (accessed 24 August 2016).

14. 'Think the EU's bad now? Wait until Albania joins: With piercing logic and passionate eloquence, Michael Gove warns that EU expansion will open our borders to 88 million from Europe's poorest countries', *Daily Mail*, 30 April 2016, http://www.dailymail.co.uk/debate/article-3566620/Michael-Gove-warns-EU-expansion-open-borders-88-million-Europe-s-poorest-countries.html (accessed 24 August 2016).

15. 'Brexit Poll Tracker', *Financial Times*, last updated 23 June 2016, https://ig.ft.com/sites/brexit-polling/

16. http://leftunity.org/brexit-and-the-rise-of-racism/ (accessed 24 August 2016).

17. Stathis Kouvelakis, 'An Open Letter to the British Left', Jacobin Mag, 7 July 2016, https://www.jacobinmag.com/2016/07/brexit-referendum-remain-leave-corbyn-racism-xenophobia-greece-austerity-eu/ (accessed 24 August 2016).

18. Yanis Varoufakis and co, 'Europe's Left after Brexit: DiEM25's perspective in reply to Tariq Ali, Stathis Kouvelakis, Vicente Navarro and Stefano Fassina', DiEM 2025, 4.

19. On this see Etienne Balibar, *We, the People of Europe?: Reflections on Transnational Citizenship*, new edition (Princeton, N.J.: Princeton University Press, 2003), 19.

20. Richard Falk, 'Resisting "globalisation-from-above" through "globalisation-from-below"', *New Political Economy* 2, no. 1 (1 March 1997), 17.

21. See the video journalism from Ash Sarkar in Barking, 'The Unbearable Whiteness of Brexit', Novara Media, no date, http://novaramedia.com/2016/07/the-unbearable-whiteness-of-brexit/ (accessed 24

August 2016), and John Harris for the *Guardian*, 'Welcome to the divided, angry Kingdom', 22 June 2016 https://www.theguardian.com/commentisfree/video/2016/jun/22/eu-referendum-welcome-to-the-divided-angry-kingdom-video (accessed 24 August 2016).

22. YouGov / Today Programme Survey Results 13 – 14 June 2016 http://d25d2506sfb94s.cloudfront.net/cumulus_uploads/document/x4iynd1mn7/TodayResults_160614_EUReferendum_W.pdf (accessed 24 August 2016).

23. 'YouGov Survey Results', 13 – 14 June 2016, http://d25d2506sfb94s.cloudfront.net/cumulus_uploads/document/463g4e5e0e/LBCResults_160614_EUReferendum_W.pdf (accessed 24 August 2016)

24. Colin Crouch, *Post-Democracy*, 1st edition (Malden, MA: Polity Press, 2004).

25. Harvey, *A Brief History of Neoliberalism*.

26. It is difficult to imagine how, for example, British trade unionists – whose right to strike will be dramatically curtailed by the Conservative government's new Trade Union Bill – could possibility represent a threat to capitalist profitability in the context of historically low levels of strike action.

27. Jürgen Habermas, *Europe: The Faltering Project* (Cambridge ; Malden, MA: Polity Press, 2009), 185 – 186.

28. 'Europe's leaders hail new currency', CNN, 1 January 2002, http://edition.cnn.com/2002/WORLD/europe/01/01/euro.reax/index.html (accessed 24 August 2016).

29. 'Greece joins eurozone', BBC, 1 January 2001, http://news.bbc.co.uk/1/hi/business/1095783.stm (accessed 24 August 2016).

30. 'The agony of Greece', *Economist*, 4 March 2015, http://www.economist.com/blogs/graphicdetail/2015/03/daily-chart-0 (accessed 24 August 2016).

31. For a very clearly written explanation of the eurozone's fiscal transfer problem vis-à-vis the United States see Krugman, P., 'The Revenge of the Optimum Currency Area', http://krugman.blogs.nytimes.com/2012/06/24/revenge-of-the-optimum-currency-area/?_r=0 (accessed 28 September 2015).

32. Ed Balls, 'Euro-monetarism: how Britain was ensnared and how it should escape', extract from Fabian Society pamphlet, June 26 1992, http://openeuropeblog.blogspot.ae/1992_06_01_archive.html (accessed 24 August 2016).

33. Perry Anderson, *The New Old World*, reprint edition (London; New York: Verso Books, 2011), 29 – 30.

34. For the statistical breakdown of the economic divide between Europe's

north and south, see: http://europeansnapshot.com/2015/09/08/ europe-grows-apart/ (accessed 28 October 2015).

35. Paul Mason, 'Greece put its faith in democracy but Europe has vetoed the result', *Guardian*, 13 July 2015, http://www.theguardian.com/ world/2015/jul/13/greece-bailout-eurozone-democracy-is-loser (accessed 28 October 2015).

36. Yanis Varoufakis, 'Modest Proposal', July 2013, https://yanisvaroufakis. eu/euro-crisis/modest-proposal/ (accessed 24 August 2016).

37. Joseph Stiglitz, 'Seven changes needed to save the euro and the EU', *Guardian*, 22 August 2016, https://www.theguardian.com/ business/2016/aug/22/seven-changes-needed-to-save-the-euro-and-the-eu?CMP=fb_gu (accessed 24 August 2016).

38. Balibar, *We, the People of Europe?*, 8.

39. Teivo Teivainen 'World Social Forum: what should it be when it grows up?', Open Democracy, 10 July 2004, https://www.opendemocracy.net/ democracy-protest/article_1342.jsp (accessed 24 August 2016).

40. For more on Another Europe Is Possible see http://www. anothereurope.org/ (accessed 24 August 2016).

41. Mary Kaldor, Sabine Selchow, and Tamsin Murray-Leach, *Subterranenan Politics in Europe* (Basingstoke: Palgrave Macmillan, 2014)

Building a more, not less, mobile world

ZOE GARDNER

For a lot of people on the progressive side of politics, the result of the June 23rd British referendum on membership of the EU was a devastating shock. For those of us who work, live and breathe as campaigners for migrant and refugee rights, it was an earthquake. A round public rejection of all of the values and arguments that we have dedicated our energy to promoting, a free-fall into uncertainty for all our future plans, and a cataclysmic blow to the stability, safety and well-being of the communities of immigrants and refugees that we work with and for. From this low point, we will have to regroup, re-energise and do much, much better to promote humane policies and convince people of the overwhelming arguments for building a more, not less, mobile world.

There is no doubt that the Leave vote was galvanised by the forces of xenophobia, racism and fear. This is not, of course, to say that all Leave-voters are racist or even that they were all motivated by a desire to decrease immigration, but for a significant majority this was, to a greater or lesser extent, the basis of their vote to leave. The campaign for Brexit was characterised by dog-whistling and outright racism and xenophobia, and the referendum result vindicated this approach and those sentiments in the minds of the anti-immigrant right. This was evidenced both in the reactions of politicians, each falling further over the last to play up their 'understanding' of voter 'concerns' around immigration, and the emboldening of racists themselves, with a significant spike in hate-crime across the country in the weeks directly after the vote, concentrated in leave-voting areas.

It's important to note here that I am using the term racism as well as xenophobia to describe this phenomenon, as the ire of the Brexit voters who turned violent was by no means confined to attacks on Poles, Romanians and other 'white European' groups in the UK who had benefited from freedom of movement, ostensibly the target of the Brexit vote. All visible minority groups experienced the rise in open expressions of hatred in the wake of the result, including minority ethnic British citizens and especially those perceived to be Muslim. This is no surprise, given that a large part of the Leave campaign intentionally 'racialised' EU immigration beyond white Christian Europeans, playing off long-standing prejudices against ethnic minority communities and Islamophobia. Farage's infamous 'Breaking Point' billboard that presented refugees seeking sanctuary in Europe as a threat is a case in point here, as was the official Leave campaign's emphasis on the 76 million (Muslim) Turks, poised to decamp imminently into our backyards as soon as they were granted free movement in the context of Turkish accession to the EU. This, of course, was not on the cards for the foreseeable future. But enough about the facts.

The mainstream Remain campaign meanwhile, responded to a referendum where the salient points of discourse were all about rejection of the elite and the establishment and anger at perceived 'uncontrolled' immigration, by putting forward a succession of increasingly elite, establishment voices advising voters not to worry about immigration, but to vote based on the economy instead. Scare stories about impending loss of influence and increasing poverty unsurprisingly did little to convince voters who already feel poor and marginalised in the first place.

With hindsight the result looks like a foregone conclu-
sion, but during the campaign we dared to hope, and we
dared to campaign and put forward a radically different vision for remaining in the EU. One that defended the rights
and benefits associated with EU membership, including an
unabashed defence of freedom of movement, but which also
demanded more, urged people to believe that we could make
our EU membership work better for them, make the EU work
better, and that it was worth staying in it to do so. We were
not successful, but we did start a conversation that is worth
continuing, one that links up with other progressive movements stretching across Europe about what kind of EU we
really want. The battle has been lost, but as the war over
what 'Brexit means Brexit' is really going to mean wages on,
there is a huge amount still left to play for. On the immigration side, we need new approaches, better, more convincing
arguments. This essay discusses some of these arguments
and positions, in the hope of continuing the conversation of
how to build a European movement that works for all people,
Brits, other EU citizens, and the rest of the world too, and
that wins the argument on global migration.

It is incredibly difficult to let go of a fact-based argument,
when the facts are on your side. It is widely accepted among experts on the subject at this point that immigration brings a net
economic benefit to the UK. This means, simply, that immigrants
pay for more of the NHS, and schools, and infrastructure than they
themselves use. Fundamentally it is down to the government to
reinvest that extra income to the benefit of the public. This has
been the crux of evidence-based pro-immigration advocacy.

There has been some uncertainty over whether immigration brings the same benefit to all parts of society, and especially some questions over whether workers at the very low
end of the income spectrum have seen some under-cutting and
therefore a slight lowering of wages, but even that has recently

been put into doubt by an LSE study[1] showing that wages at the lower end of the spectrum have stagnated equally, if not more so, in areas with low immigration, as where it is high, suggesting that immigration has not been a factor.

Generally, those relying on the evidence are able to conclude that inequality, which sky-rocketed in the 80s, has never been adequately addressed since then, leaving long-term patterns of deprivation in certain sectors and regions which have little to do with immigration. Wages were depressed for many in the aftermath of the 2008 financial crisis and have not recovered, again, in patterns that cannot satisfactorily be linked to immigration.

Despite this, we have seen time and time again, and most starkly during the referendum campaign, how the facts don't work. People do not want to hear or believe statistics that go against what they perceive as 'the evidence of their own eyes' and a narrative brought to them on repeat by sources that they trust such as the tabloid press and Nigel Farage. None of this however, lets the mainstream Remain campaign or anyone else off the hook for refusing to engage adequately with the question of immigration during the campaign. There *are* positive ways of talking about immigration that could have gone a significant way towards changing attitudes, perhaps not among the decidedly racist, but among those whose human compassion for immigrants and refugees is simply being displaced by fears for the wellbeing of their own families and communities that they connect with 'over population' and a resultant strain on public services.

The reintroduction of a migrant impact fund would have been (and still must be) the first positive proposal to make as regards alleviating people's concerns over infrastructure in areas seeing high influxes of immigrants. The fund, which previ-

---

1. Wadsworth, J. & Ottaviano, G., *Brexit and the Impact of Immigration on the UK*, Centre for Economic Performance, London School of Economics, Brexit Paper 05, http://cep.lse.ac.uk/pubs/download/brexit05.pdf

ously saw the light of day briefly, introduced by Gordon Brown in 2008 and scrapped without ceremony by the coalition government in 2010, was paid for by an additional £50 levy introduced on visa fees to enter the UK, meaning it was paid for by immigrants themselves (although not EU immigrants, who do not require a visa). This levy, it may be noted, did not face the axe along with the fund when it went.

A dedicated pot of money, paid for by immigration (although the method to achieve this could be re-examined), that can be used by councils specifically to address pressure on local school places, housing lists and hospitals is an obvious way of better managing the impact in areas where rates of immigration are high. It recognises the fact that an influx of people to an area, wherever they come from, will create new infrastructure needs within that community; it promotes regional and localised control over spending priorities, which can increase trust and transparency; it can promote inclusion and integration between communities; and as a rhetorical device, it responds in a meaningful way to those who argue their communities are 'overwhelmed' by new arrivals and 'left behind' by central government.

Evidence from the referendum results shows, in a pattern that echoes analysis of where UKIP votes have been strongest in recent years, that it is not the areas with the highest immigrant populations that voted leave, far from it, but areas where there has been a rapid growth in the rate of immigration, even in comparatively low numbers. This makes the argument for a migrant impact fund yet more compelling, as it would be specifically targeted towards addressing the issues that come about, in the comparatively short term, in such areas.

Another fundamental prong to any defence of freedom of movement should have been (and still should be) to take labour exploitation much more seriously. Under EU rules it should not be possible for employers to discriminate between EU nationals in the work place, whether they are British or Polish. This ought to mean that workers of all nationalities receive the same minimum pay and conditions in any industry. There is, of course, evidence that this is not always the case, with stories of Eastern Europeans in particular being prepared to work 'for peanuts' at the expense of British workers dominating tabloid headlines. Immigrants, even EU nationals with the legal right to work on the same level as British citizens are often at the sharp end of labour exploitation, sowing divisions and resentment among fellow workers.

However, there is a much wider problem of exploitative working conditions across the country, as the recent revelations about 'Victorian workhouse'-style conditions at Sports Direct have made all too clear. It was fascinating to me to hear the interviews of Sports Direct workers after the scandal came to light, and how one after the other they asserted that yes, it was hard, but they had worked in places where conditions were worse. It is indeed inconceivable that Sports Direct is the only major employer in the country that is routinely flouting basic minimum standards and wage conditions for workers; we should be calling for a government inquiry into working conditions across the board. Any defence of freedom of movement for EU workers cannot be decoupled from a campaign to investigate exploitative working conditions for all parts of the country. If minimum (or even living) wages and conditions were actively enforced, it would go a long way to address the resentment and insecurity on the part of working communities that has so successfully been turned against immigrants in recent decades. It goes without saying of course that improving conditions for all workers is also a good end in its own right for us on the left.

These, among others, are strong, left-wing and principled arguments and policies that can be put forward in defence of freedom of movement and its benefits for ordinary Brits that do not rely on saying 'no, you're wrong, here's a bunch of numbers'. We should be advancing these positions at every chance we get. It is a shameful misjudgement on the part of many politicians to capitulate to baseless anti-immigrant rhetoric, or to brush the whole question aside, as if it is an inconvenient truth, a point we cannot possibly win.

One of the most disingenuous arguments put forward by Leavers, and picked up on by many 'Lexiters' brings me to the other major immigration issue that we need to tackle – and get hold of the narrative on – as a matter of absolute urgency: refugees. It is argued by many, that EU freedom of movement represents the privileging of (mainly white) European workers over people from the rest of the world and notably the Global South. EU immigration policy is characterised as racist and divisive, a project aimed at ring-fencing our riches, and the enriching benefits of immigration, to our continent alone, while the rest of the world loses out.

Of course the solution to this is not found by removing freedom of movement rights from everybody in order to level the playing field at the lowest common denominator; it lies rather in extending the ways in which non-Europeans are able to benefit from migration too. Let us be clear: the very wealthy, no matter where they're from, have seen a huge increase in their ability to migrate over recent decades. A very rich person from any country may be able to obtain the education and skills necessary to fulfil even the UK's stringent visa requirements, and pay the cost of obtaining said visa and moving here. An extremely rich person doesn't even need to worry about the skills part, you do not need a job offer, or even to have any command of the English language to come here if you can show that you have enough money in the bank to make a significant investment in UK business. Meanwhile if you are poor, unskilled and from the Global South, there are no pathways to legal migration to Europe.

EU freedom of movement has meant that less well-off Europeans have been able to benefit from migration in a way that for the rest of the world is only open to the rich. One need only look at Chancellor Philip Hammond's recent pledge to retain the benefits of freedom of movement beyond Brexit exclusively for employees of the City of London to see the direction that those who would remove free movement for the rest of us are looking to move in: they want to price poor Europeans out of the opportunities provided by international mobility as they have done the poor of the rest of the world.

If national borders are increasingly disappearing for big business and for the world's rich, the 'refugee crisis' is the flipside. Those of us who can flash the right passport or the right wad of cash can travel with so few limitations these days, while borders, ever more visible and deadly, are all too real for those who can't. On-going attempts to clamp down on undocumented travel towards Europe have created a dangerous and unsustainable situation in which people fleeing poverty and persecution are trapped at Europe's doorstep, relying on smugglers and risking their lives in ever-more-risky attempts to reach our streets. There is a consistent narrative in the EU institutions that these stringent external border controls are what safeguards support for liberal migration policies on the inside. We must stand utterly opposed to this logic, which at any rate has manifestly proven itself to be false.

The EU's abject failure to find solutions to the refugee crisis of the last 18 months that are either humane or at all credible is matched only by the failure of the UK government to do the same. Prime Minister Theresa May, architect of the 'hostile environment' for undocumented migrants while Home Secretary, has a history of scapegoating refugees in her repeated attempts to be viewed as 'tough' on immigration. By any measure, this does not make sense: refugees are not only the most vulnerable of all immigrant groups, but they also make up just 6% of immigration flows to this country, so they're hardly a practical choice to target if the desire truly is to bring down net inflows 'to the tens of thousands', as has been May's stated aim.

In response to a referendum vote that will be taken as a cry for more 'tough measures' on immigration, refugees and asylum seekers are likely to continue to be placed at the front line by this government. The 'Breaking Point' poster that suggested voting Leave would insulate the UK from refugee flows is a case in point here: anti-immigrant sentiment is, as noted above, not actually about mere 'control' – our strict asylum procedure is the definition of a controlled immigration route. It is for far too many about 'fewer foreigners' and most definitely fewer Muslims and people of colour. Of course our obligations towards refugees stem from international law, although some of it is codified at the EU level; so Brexit will fortunately not relieve the UK of the responsibility to provide protection to those fleeing persecution. However, Theresa May is already testing some messages around weakening refugee protection that have been shown to be effective and dangerous.

A note on the legal definition of a refugee: many progressives argue convincingly that the definition of a refugee under the law is too narrow, including people fleeing persecution and violence, but not those fleeing poverty and the effects of climate change. It is reasonable to argue that a person escaping starvation should be entitled to move and set up a life in another country, just as a person escaping war should. I agree with this argument, just as I agree that all people, not only Europeans, should ideally be able to benefit from freedom of movement. And my response is the same: we need to defend at all costs what we have got, and then seek to extend it. By discrediting the mobility rights that we have already secured for some groups, we will only achieve a weakening of those rights, not a reciprocal increase in the rights of others. I will defend to the death an asylum system that saves thousands of people, year on year, from the torture chambers of some of the world's most horrific regimes, even if it fails abjectly to protect other people from poverty. For that we must seek new ways.

For realism's sake, this comes down to making the case for an unskilled immigration route to the UK and the EU. The refugee crisis has shown us that it is unfeasible to prevent undocumented migration completely, nor are the methods required to attempt it acceptable by any moral standard. In the long term, the fences around our rich countries will fall and it is only by building pathways to greater global mobility that we will begin to manage the reality of that future. This must still be better framed than it has yet been; it would be refreshing to hear a politician admit that the only way to prevent dangerous, chaotic and uncontrolled undocumented journeys into the UK, clinging to the bottom of lorries, or hiding out in shipping containers, is to provide an alternative route. This would satisfy the desire for 'control', as all applicants would be vetted via the visa application system, but would also destroy the business model of smugglers, who rely on the desperation of those who have no other means to travel but are absolutely determined to do so. Give those people a safe and legal option.

This is an area where, possibly more than any other, we will fail if we attempt to do it alone. The UK couldn't feasibly enact a truly humane, considered and far more open immigration and asylum strategy without a similar approach across Europe. On too small a scale, this has already been demonstrated by Germany over the past year. Instead of following the German lead, each welcoming and regularising the asylum seekers arriving in their territories, other countries simply waved a million refugees onwards into Germany, in a march of desperation across the continent. This was a derogation of duty on behalf of surrounding member states that has massively contributed to the abject situation for refugees across the continent today.

Much of what I have argued here relates to the need to push power down to the regional and local level, allowing communities more involvement and control of budgets and policies that affect them directly to ensure ordinary people's buy-in and understanding, and the better sharing of the positive impacts of immigration among them. But we must look outwards internationally too, the left in Britain must do more to build bridges with like-minded movements across the European region and beyond if progressive voices are to get a fair hearing in the wider migration debate. We must join up with European counterparts to demand real solutions from EU leaders on refugees. Not another wall that redirects people to a more dangerous alternative route; not another pay-off to unsavoury regimes in developing countries to contain refugees and migrants; we need new solutions, flexible realistic and long-term solutions that make the most out of human mobility.

Beyond this we must reach out across sectors too, combine the insights of experts on housing, social and environmental policy, employment rights and welfare among others with those of immigration specialists to ensure that our proposals are consistent and that these areas do not develop policy proposals without a good understanding of how to make migration work within them.

For too long migrants' rights campaigners have been hamstrung by concerns about wading out of our area of expertise and commenting authoritatively on the effects of austerity, job insecurity, the housing crisis and the lack of investment in key infrastructure areas as major causes of anti-immigrant feeling across Europe. Rather than remaining silo-ed, we must build better coalitions of campaigners on the left who are able to speak to the inter-connected nature of all these struggles for dignity. While people's real concerns centre around the need for more investment in public services and secure, dignified work, we cannot simply stand on the edge of these issues and say that 'it's not the immigrants' fault'. We need to provide better answers, and we need to be finding those answers with input from both British and immigrant voices.

At the very least this will require a concerted effort to hold all MPs, but particularly those in the progressive opposition parties, to account over giving way to misplaced scapegoating of immigration for the exclusion of Britain's 'left behind' communities. Giving ground to lies about immigration in the hope of chasing the votes of those who opted for leave is a cowardly and destructive spiral that will only strengthen the reactionary right's position on Brexit. We must use our influence, wherever we have it, to ensure this backsliding does not continue. We must arm those willing to make the case for immigration with practical and positive solutions, with the rhetorical strength to win through in a field of misinformation, knee-jerk racism and prejudice.

An essay such as this can necessarily only scratch the surface of what needs to be done to combat the current climate of hostility towards immigration and refugees and the negative impact it has on local and global communities. A long-term vision for global mobility that takes into account the real needs of local people alongside the wider on-going cultural fight against institutional racism and individual prejudice will need to be developed as a fundamental part of our struggle in the months and years to come.

Most importantly we must not surrender in the wake of the referendum result. We must not roll over and accept defeat on the case for immigration, nor allow our political representatives to do so. If a hard Brexit is pursued and immigrants continue to be targeted, it is the very people who voted Leave because they were 'left behind' who will feel the most severe economic impact. There will still be immigrants and Muslims to lay the blame on when that happens, so we must be prepared with a more effective alternative narrative of our own. The Brexit vote must be a galvanising moment for everyone who believes in the fundamental equality and worth of all people, regardless of socio-economic status or nationality, to mainstream these ideas into a politics that works emphatically for all.

Zoe Gardner is a PhD researcher on migrant and refugee journeys at the London School of Economics. She has worked at refugee-assisting NGOs in London and Brussels and is an active campaigner for refugee and migrants' rights.

After Brexit: reckoning with Britain's racism and xenophobia

LALEH KHALILI

Theoretically, there was a progressive case to be made for Britain exiting the European Union via the referendum held on June 23, 2016. But the campaign for Brexit – the infelicitous name given the political process – was, from the very first, fought on the grounds of xenophobia and racism. Moreover, what has transpired in Britain since the Leave campaign won has only shown how easily the veneer of civility and conviviality can be peeled back to reveal the virulence of racism and xenophobia seething under the skin of British social life.

Britain was never a part of the eurozone. Therefore, the extensive austerity measures that its Tory/Liberal Democrat coalition government of 2010-2015 put into place, and that the Tory government of 2015 ratcheted up, were its own doing. That said, the austerity measures emanating from the more financially powerful EU states – Germany and France – and imposed upon and massively affecting the economies of countries such as Greece and Portugal were on the forefront of every British progressive's mind before the EU referendum. It is possible to be a member of the EU and not part of the eurozone monetary sphere – as is the case with the UK, alongside Bulgaria, Croatia, Czech Republic, Denmark, Hungary, Poland, Romania and Sweden.

The EU itself is a massive bureaucratic mechanism, institutional machine and ideological apparatus devised to facilitate the movement of capital, goods, services and people across its internal borders. The free – or relatively unrestricted – movement of goods and capital without encountering tariffs or protection barriers has resulted in the further consolidation of the power of the big manufacturers in Europe as well as unfettered growth in and institutional protection of the financial and banking sector. The EU legal bodies legislate around or regulate some of this free trade, but generally decide in favour of big business over trade unions.

The EU's 'empire of free trade' has been the target of the ire of both the right and the left; the right is incensed over the regulations seen to hamper businesses (especially environmental and health-and-safety regulations as well as the human rights charter) and the left is incensed over the unaccountability of the EU officials and its rigid neoliberal stance. This undemocratic power exercised by distant Eurocrats is the plausible basis of a progressive criticism of the institution.

But what has distinguished the EU free-trade pact from other free-trade pacts – notably the North American Free Trade Agreement – is the relatively unrestricted movement of people across internal European borders to seek jobs or residency elsewhere in the Union. And it is this free movement of people that has triggered a long-festering xenophobia at the heart of British society.

Britain's insularity has been punctured throughout its history in moments where the need for migrant labour has trumped the Little Englander aversion toward foreigners. One such moment was the post-Second World War reconstruction era when the devastated country needed people to aid in the reconstruction of the national economy (much like the rest of Europe). The importation of guest workers from the colonies, followed by decolonization and the migration of former colonized subjects to the metropole has triggered virulent xenophobic and racist responses in Britain. That the British political classes have refused to reckon with the country's colonial legacy and their steadfast refusal to acknowledge the racism interwoven in its institutions have only exacerbated this xenophobia and racism.

This xenophobia takes different shapes according to the historical moment, but neoliberal policies have only ever intensified these sentiments. Migrants are today blamed for taking up places in housing and schools, burdening the country's publicly-funded universal health system and weakening the working class. Scant attention is paid to how, beginning with Margaret Thatcher's scorched-earth neoliberalism, policies of privatization and austerity – during both feast and famine – have led to a degradation of national life, a diminishing of social mobility and a growth in inequality in the UK.

In the 1990s, under the reign of Tony Blair's New Labour, Thatcher's policies continued in new guises: the fiercely beloved National Health Service (NHS) was funded, but often via public-private partnerships that have in fact burdened the NHS with serious debt and crumbling infrastructures while enriching private investors and developers. Instead of preserving unused schools, local councils were encouraged to sell off their school buildings in the 1990s, again benefiting property developers who turned these attractive Victorian structures into high-end housing without anticipating the acute future need for school buildings and school places. The sale of social housing, which had been a pillar of Thatcherite policy of privatization, has been exacerbated by wholly inadequate construction of new affordable housing and no effort to replace the stock of social housing lost under Thatcher.

The privatization of the efficient national rail, electricity, phone and water infrastructures has been a boon to profiteering private firms, while the basic transport and utility infrastructures have deteriorated, and their costs – especially of commuting – have become exorbitant. The replacement of manufacturing jobs with service jobs, the destruction of the mining and shipping sectors, and the weakening of trade union protections – particularly in the more militant sectors – have also had massively detrimental effects on vast swathes of Britain's industrial areas.

It is no matter that the Tory Party (under its official name the Conservatives) is ostensibly a party of both fiscal and social conservatism, that the Liberal Democrats are ostensibly a party of social liberalism and fiscal conservatism, and that Labour is a self-avowed socialist party (though subjected to neoliberal reforms under Tony Blair, New Labour moved to the centre as did many other social democratic parties in Europe). In the face of rising popular discontent with this abasement of social life in the UK, it has been easier for politicians across the political spectrum to displace the blame for these policies to vulnerable migrants rather than to acknowledge the role not only of the Conservative Party (and for a while, its Liberal Democrat coalition partners), but also of the Labour Party in bringing about this turn of events. In this regard, Labour has been wholly complicit in pandering to xenophobic sentiments in order to deflect blame from New Labour policies.

These policies of austerity and attendant anti-migrant sentiments have occurred in the context of ever more intense hysteria around the question of 'terror'. We live in a time of legislations on radicalization, particularly the absurdly authoritarian 'Prevent' laws, practices of surveillance not only of Muslims, but also of 'suspicious' talk in schools, universities, hospitals and public places, and counterterrorism operations. These government measures – and particularly the Prevent legislation, which makes it mandatory for school and university teachers to spy on their students and any public official to look out for signs of 'radicalization' among Muslim youths in particular – have led to criminalization of entire communities, and an increase in the sense of vulnerability among British citizens and residents of Muslim origin.

This convergence of anti-migrant xenophobia and Islamophobic racism has now become the most recognizable feature of politics in Britain and has shaped successive election campaigns. Parliamentary elections, especially since 2010, have often pivoted around the question of migration. Although in the 2015 elections, Nigel Farage's right-wing anti-immigration and Eurosceptic UK Independence Party (UKIP), only secured one seat in parliament, he nevertheless picked up millions of votes and Farage managed to define the discourse around migration. So much so, that in pandering to UKIP's base, David Cameron announced the EU referendum.

The London mayoral election, held a scant eight weeks before the EU referendum, was another example of this ignominious turn. The campaign between Labour's Sadiq Khan, a liberal Muslim leaning toward New Labour, and the Tories' Zac Goldsmith, until then best known for his environmental campaigning, showed the extent to which even the more ostensibly liberal members of the Tory Party would appeal to this seam of racism and Islamophobia in order to win votes. This all came to a head with the referendum, where all other issues faded into the background and migration and anti-Muslim sentiments (the latter of which does not have a logical relation to the EU in any case) became the central axis around which the referendum pivoted.

Although the outcome was not really foreseen, and although the end result of the referendum was fairly close (52 percent for Leave; 48 percent for Remain), the win for the Eurosceptics took even Leave voters by surprise.

The most prevalent cliché of post-referendum analysis has been that the vote for exit should be read as a 'working-class revolt'. Setting aside the unspoken assumption that this rebellious working class must by definition be white, the post-referendum exit polls actually indicate the 'working-class' characterization of the Leave vote is inaccurate. It is true that a higher percentage of working-class voters voted for exit than did upper- and middle-class voters – 64 percent versus 46 percent. But once turnout by class was taken into account, the numbers looked different. As Ben Pritchett's calculations (along with his caveats about the turnout numbers including anomalies) have shown, the far greater turnout of the middle and upper classes, versus the working class - 90 percent versus 52 percent - meant that in absolute numbers, a far higher number of middle- and upper-class voters (around 10 million voters) actually voted to leave the EU than the working class (approximately 7 million voters), many others of whom abstained from voting.

Lord Ashcroft's exit polls showed that if voters thought that multiculturalism, feminism, social liberalism, the environmental movement and immigration are forces for ill, they voted overwhelmingly to leave the EU. The same polls showed that while 53 percent of voters who described themselves as white and 58 percent of those who described themselves as Christian voted to leave the EU, more than two-thirds of Asian voters, nearly three-quarters of Black voters and 70 percent of self-identified Muslims voted to remain in the EU.

Only hours after their win, the Eurosceptic leaders had already back-pedalled on some of their most major promises. Nigel Farage claimed that he never agreed with the claim - emblazoned on the side of a campaign bus used by Eurosceptic leaders - that the £350 million weekly payments formerly paid to the EU would actually be used to fund the NHS. Iain Duncan Smith's weaker claim was that only after the EU agricultural subsidies (to the Tory heartlands) were replaced would any leftover funds be divided between the NHS and other needs. The irony was of course that many of those agricultural heartlands had been in receipt of more handouts from the EU than other places in the UK.

Claims that the UK fisheries could benefit from a post-EU deregulation were similarly walked back. Even on migration, which had played such a decisive and divisive role in the referendum, the Eurosceptic leaders were already tempering their claims. These retreats from promises have been so blatant that the Leave campaign has simply wiped the archive of all their opinion pieces and documents from the web.

Even more astonishing is how the Leave camp seems not to have planned at all for an eventual exit. There is no certainty as to when – or even whether – Article 50 (a provision of the Treaty of Lisbon which provides for EU member countries leaving) will ever be invoked, setting into motion two years of negotiations that will allow Britain to unravel its legislations, trade arrangements, migration processes and regulations from the EU.

Perhaps the most worrying fallout of the referendum vote, however, has been the extraordinary spike in violence against migrants and non-white British citizens and residents. Although many – if not most – of those who voted for Leave did not do so out of xenophobic or racist reasons, the vote seems to have legitimated an extraordinary outburst of such attacks against migrants – especially those from Poland – and non-white British citizens, residents and visitors.

There is very little that promises an abatement of such racism. The immediate economic fallout of the Leave vote will only exacerbate the sense of economic uncertainty, possibly leading to a recession. The weakening of the pound will inevitably lead to a rise in the price of imports (which will be exacerbated by the implementation of tariffs once the UK leaves the EU). Massive losses in the stock market have wiped vast amounts off pensions, giving yet more alibis to the state and private pension providers for reducing what is available to retirees. Rating agencies' downgrading of the UK's ability to borrow will lead to higher borrowing costs for the UK government and a growth in the UK deficit, which of course provides an excuse for further austerity measures and an increase in taxes (which Tory governments of course will not levy against the corporations or the richest earners). The revocation of

EU protections for migrant workers means that while the UK will continue to see migration from the EU countries, these workers will not be protected from the worst depredations of unscrupulous employers. As labour studies scholar Roland Erne has argued, this degradation of migrant worker rights will only accelerate the race to the bottom for *all workers*, both migrant and British. Nor will parliamentary politics in England provide any respite.

Already, politicians from Scotland and Northern Ireland (both of which voted overwhelmingly to remain in the EU) are talking of a second independence referendum and a reunification of Ireland, respectively, in order to remain in the EU. The rump state that would remain if such fragmentation occurred would likely have a much strengthened Tory government and a Labour Party that would have difficulty winning.

In a coming recession, with intensified inequality, rising poverty and stalled social mobility, under a Tory government which has no stakes in egalitarian social policies, racism and xenophobia, right-wing populism, ultranationalist ideologies, even fascism will find a fertile soil. The horrifying racist and xenophobic attacks of recent months are haunted by the 'rivers of blood' racism of yesteryear. In a now notorious 1968 speech, the Tory MP Enoch Powell promised rivers of blood to a country in which migration had led to 'the black man [having] the whip hand over the white man'. UKIP's Nigel Farage has never hidden his admiration for Enoch Powell, and even the anti-immigrant views of many in the Tory Party are shaped by Powell.

The long and brutal history of British colonialism and empire lies at the heart of so much British insularity and racism. The deep roots of this racism will likely influence the politics of tomorrow, as it has already done that of today. To counter such a bleak future, mass mobilization is necessary – and any form of progressive mass mobilization has to recognize that class politics are always articulated through a politics of race.

Reckoning with Britain's racism and xenophobia across time, place, parties and social classes is the necessary first step in such mobilization.

Laleh Khalili teaches politics at SOAS, University of London.

Brexit and the need for a left internationalist trade policy

NICK DEARDEN

Trade is always about power. That's why, in post-Brexit Britain, trade deals will be at the centre of the most important question we face. These deals will in effect embed our new constitution, detailing how we approach issues like immigration, food policy, finance and public services.

Theoretically, Brexit could lead to British governments developing more progressive relationships with countries of the developing and developed world. But there are serious obstacles confronting us. First, in the case of a 'hard Brexit', that the very fact of our exit from the EU will impose competitive pressures to which the most obvious answer will be lower regulation, lower wages, lower taxes. Second, that successive British governments have in any case shown a preference for these policies, and the current government contains the most dogmatic pro-liberalisation and deregulation ministers in modern history.

But a third problem is that the left, more used to fighting against trade deals we don't like, has little understanding of what 'good trade' means. If we are not to repeat the experience of the referendum – a battle between right and further right – we must urgently create a vision of trade which resonates with

British people, providing a positive route out of the crisis of which Brexit is a symptom.

WHY TRADE?

Trade is not simply a system for exchanging goods with other countries, but the lynchpin of the global economic system. What we trade, how we trade it and with whom – whether you're selling spices, or even people, in the eighteenth century, or fruit, cars or money itself today – is central to understanding economic power.

That's why, while few people cited trade directly in Britain's EU referendum campaign, the issues of immigration, of deindustrialisation, of public services, of financial power and inequality – all directly relate to the global 'trade' system we live under. That's why trade will be at the centre of the Brexit negotiations over the next few years. The type of deals Britain signs will dictate much of what our economy looks like.

There is a popular understanding of this importance of trade – witness the huge pan-European movement against mega corporate trade deals like TTIP (the Transatlantic Trade & Investment Partnership between the US and EU).

But while it is left-wing forces that have come close to defeating TTIP, in the wake of both Brexit in the UK and the Trump phenomenon in the US, it is the right that leads the debate on trade – from the free market fundamentalists in Theresa May's government to the hardline protectionists on Trump's team.

The reason can be traced back to the capitulation of social democracy to neoliberalism in the 1990s, leaving today's left lacking a clearly articulated alternative which would resonate with its base in *either* the internationalist remain camp or the protectionist leave camp – let alone both. We urgently need a clear left wing strategy and vision for a trade system which promotes more democratic public services, improves social and environmental protection, *and* which preserves and expands free movement of people and genuine regional and international cooperation.

FROM CHIAPAS TO SEATTLE

It is not impossible to both oppose globalisation – the system of neoliberal economics that has grown up since the mid 1970s – and to build a progressive international economy beyond the nation state. The heyday of opposition to free trade in the late 1990s made just such an assumption – opposition, while locally anchored, was inherently internationalist in its outlook.

The opening shots of that resistance were fired by the army of the Zapatistas on New Year's Day 1994. The Zapatistas were rightly concerned that the North American Free Trade Agreement (NAFTA), which came into force that day, would wipe out peasant farmers, and force them into sweatshops along the US border. NAFTA represented a commodification of the social transactions which had preserved life in rural Mexico for centuries.

The anti-globalisation movement brought together liberals, socialists, anarchists, environmentalists and feminists in a diverse movement which attempted to reinvent a democratic left-wing politics following the fall of soviet communism. At the centre of the struggle was 'free trade', that universal 'good' which became a vehicle for the limitless expansion of corporate power into every corner of our lives.

The Multilateral Agreement on Investment – the TTIP of its day – attempted to secure new legal privileges for 'investors'. It was beaten, in one of the first global campaigns to utilise the internet, in just 18 months.

The 'Battle in Seattle' fought off northern countries which were attempting to write the same rules in the World Trade Organisation. Resistance, again, brought it to a decade-long standstill.

The campaign for access to AIDS medication tried to undo the new intellectual property regime which had created global corporate monopolies responsible for suffering and death on a massive scale. The campaign saw a relaxation in intellectual property which allowed for the manufacture of generic drugs at more affordable prices.

The anti-globalisation movement is often condemned as having failed to turn the tide on corporate globalisation. This is an underestimate of what it achieved in the years before Bush and Blair declared war on the Middle East. At the high point of neoliberalism, the movement managed to expose the lies around corporate globalisation, shining a light on the institutions that had been created to govern this economy (the G8, WTO, IMF, World Bank).

What's more, it did this while remaining outward-looking, and driven by an international solidarity which is, in practice, missing from today's left.

Unfortunately social democrats didn't listen. Their conversion to neoliberalism, especially acute under Clinton and Blair, led the centre-left to see free trade not simply as a necessary evil but as a key mechanism for making the poor richer (and making the rich richer too!). This hollowing out of social democracy is central to understanding the weakness of the centre-left all across Europe and the US today. It meant that parties based on labour lost the trust of their base. Bearable in a relatively high growth economy, this tension reached breaking point after the financial crisis of 2008.

What's more, it left social democracy without positive ideas for remaking the world. In the west, no trace of an alternative trade policy now remains. It must be reinvented – and fast.

THE NEW TRADE OFFENSIVE

Of course, neoliberalism didn't stand still in the years after the anti-globalisation movement. The liberalisation agenda continued, in a piecemeal fashion. Then, in the early 2010s, we faced a new all-out offensive on the part of capital.

Big business had given up on the WTO as a space to 'get things done'. Not just the pink tide governments of Latin America, but China and India proved hostile to a neoliberal agenda dominated by the west. So a new strategy was adopted – a series of four massive deals which would incorporate everything big business had sought for 20 years, locking together to cover vast swathes of the world while excluding the west's primary competitors China, India and Russia.

The Transpacific Partnership (TPP) covers pacific rim countries from the US, Japan and Australia to Vietnam, Chile and Peru. The Transatlantic Partnership (TTIP) comprises the US and EU. CETA covers the EU and Canada. And the Trade in Services Agreement (TISA) includes 50 countries – from the US and EU countries to Pakistan and Costa Rica, and covers the 'services' sector – from finance to transport to energy to education.

Taken together, this was the biggest corporate offensive since the heyday of the anti-globalisation movement. And the core of these deals wasn't the removal of tariffs and quotas, rather it harked back to the more ambitious agenda which had been unsuccessfully pursued at the WTO 15 years earlier. Overcoming socially-inclined laws and regulations was at the centre of the agenda.

Consider laws against antibiotic usage in meat production, or minimum wage legislation, or local government using procurement budgets to stimulate local business, or rules to undermine the creation of dangerous financial derivatives. From the perspective of transnational capital, these rules are simply impediments to its ability to generate greater profits. They mean business has to operate different standards in different places. From a big business point of view, local differences should be swept away – they simply represent disguised protectionism.

The same thinking is applied to public services. Some of these deals employ mechanisms known as 'standstill' and 'ratchet' clauses which effectively dictate that any moves a government makes with regard to the public sector need to be in the direction of more liberalisation (making rules at least as advantageous to transnational capital as to, say, a local business).

In a nutshell, these corporate trade deals try to look at every aspect of society as if the only thing that mattered was the interests of international capital. They include giving business a 'right' to be involved in writing legislation and challenging 'un-necessary' regulatory burdens on them. They are also enforce-able – unlike most environmental and human rights treaties. And this enforceability is helped by allowing foreign capital special legal mechanisms to sue governments for laws which damage their 'investment'.

In reality, these mechanisms, which exist in many bilateral trade agreements, have allowed big business to sue govern-ments for putting cigarettes in plain packaging, for raising the minimum wage, for applying better health and safety standards to coal-fired power stations, and much besides. In the last 15 years a legal industry has grown up pushing the limits of what's possible under these corporate courts, in particular in stretch-ing the often used rule of 'indirect expropriation of assets', to mean virtually anything a corporation doesn't like.

Finally, these deals have been carried out behind closed doors, with little to no public information. While the European Parliament *can* stop deals on our behalf, they can't amend them, and they have never, to date, actually halted such a deal. To cap it all, no government could realistically withdraw from these deals, as they include sunset clauses of 20 years – far beyond the lifetime of most governments.

#NOTTIP

Despite the problems of these deals, campaigners didn't ex-pect the outpouring of concern witnessed over the last 2 years. That's because trade deals are notoriously dry subjects, and the narrative of 'trade means growth means jobs' is a strong one.

Success was based on the fact that campaigns were based around how the trade deals would affect people directly. In Ger-many, where TTIP is a household word, the idea of American food practices was used to build opposition. In the UK, dangers to the NHS were prioritised. In the US, senators like Elizabeth Warren focussed on the EU's financial regulation and offshoring of jobs. Southern country resistance has focussed on the price of medicines, as TPP threatens to import higher US intellectual property regulations.

This has built a campaign which has significantly held up a group of deals which were supposed to be signed and sealed by now. Indeed, there's every chance that this movement will put a permanent spanner in the works of the deals as a whole. In Europe, one year on from the campaign being launched, a record-breaking 3.2million people had signed up to stop TTIP and CETA.

This is part of a wave of resistance which has rocked the establishment to its core. See the way, in the US presidential election, in which free trader Clinton had to express her own doubts about TPP and TTIP standing, as she did, between firm opponents to the left (Bernie Saunders) and right (Donald Trump).

Even under Clinton, there would have been little future for a corporate trade offensive. We know Trump prefers bilateral deals, even more skewed to US interests. TTIP now appears dead – sacrificed by German and French social democrats in order to save the less controversial CETA, and to improve their electoral chances in 2017.

BREXIT AND TRADE

The trade campaign started as a left-wing initiative. But its power was recognised by the far right. In Britain, UKIP quickly moved from tacit support of TTIP, to all-out opposition, recognising the impact it could have on the EU referendum. They were right – while not a major factor in the vote, TTIP was used among certain audiences to help Brexit. In the US, Trump is a now major proponent of economic nationalism. He regularly denigrates trade deals like TPP. In continental Europe, virtually all far right parties have joined the anti-TTIP bandwagon too.

Although many of us who opposed TTIP argued passionately that remaining inside the EU was the best way to defeat it – and prevent free trade fundamentalists taking full control of Britain – there are undoubtedly similarities in the movement against TTIP and the vote for Brexit. Both are a reaction to the way that the free trade agenda, in its widest sense, has empowered corporations at the expense of people and democracy. Both herald the demise of neoliberalism.

But the problem facing the left in Britain – as well as in the US and EU – is that this rupture will only open up progressive potential if the left can lay out a real alternative which definitively breaks with social democracy's embrace of neoliberalism.

They will face a government which is trying to straddle a neoliberal economic policy with nationalist political rhetoric. Economically all of the main 'Brexiteers' are staunchly free market. The International Trade Secretary Liam Fox has called for a return to the 'Victorian buccaneering spirit' of Britain, which should send a shudder down the spine of anyone who understands Britain's imperial history. He told parliament recently that he wants a 'low tax, low regulation' country, clearly aiming to outcompete the EU with the lowest standards and taxes in the western world.

This is a vision which many in the financial sector *could* get behind. Sure, they'd lose market and jobs to Frankfurt in terms of eurozone trading. But they would quickly find a new role trading the sorts of products not allowed elsewhere. Combined with the right deals with China and other emerging economies, London could emerge as a primary western trading location for emerging market currencies, stocks and other financial products – no questions asked.

Foreign Secretary Boris Johnson says that the TTIP-style Canadian deal (CETA) should be a model for our future trading relations. Meanwhile, the progressive elements of the EU – freedom of movement, some social and environmental protection and cooperation – are jettisoned, consistent with the long-held view of an element of the British ruling class that has always seen Brussels as 'too socialist'.

The government will undoubtedly try to sign the fourth

TTIP-style deal, TISA, the trade in services agreement. This super-privatisation deal covers all services, from finance to telecommunications, transport to healthcare and education. From what we know about the negotiations, the deal will include a 'ratchet' clause, making renationalisation of services virtually impossible. It also threatens to prevent tighter financial regulation, obstruct governments' preferencing renewable energy, and remove the right of certain categories of immigrants from receiving labour rights. Ministers must be salivating.

The momentum behind a hard Brexit – with no institutional relationship with the EU – is building. This is the surest route to the so-called 'Singapore option', turning Britain into an offshore haven for capital. Britain's international relations would be a series of ultra-free trade deals which would see the global South producing everything we consume, paid for by the speculation and rent which form the basis of our economy.

None of this should cause us to ignore the real contradictions in the right's post-Brexit strategy. Even within the ranks of the Tory Brexiters, there *are* serious fractures which can be exploited. Theresa May's speech to the 2016 Conservative Party Conference made clear signals that the free market had failed, state intervention was back on the table, tight control of borders non-negotiable. This points to a fundamentally different strategy of economic nationalism, more familiar to Marine Le Pen: hyper-protectionism and the sort of 'beggar-my-neighbour' trade policies which grew up in the 1930s.

Currently these ideas also sit together within UKIP, and indeed within Donald Trump's administration, with little exposure from the outside world. But, if exposed in a responsible manner, they open up a real opportunity for the opposition to exploit.

DAMAGE LIMITATION

To date, the left has failed to make much dent in the debate. Unless it can begin to do so fast, our constitution will be rewritten by probably the most right-wing government in modern British history, which will deregulate, privatise and liberalise, while keeping a good portion of the working class on board with anti-immigrant policies.

What should we be arguing for? Short term the best way to protect moderate standards of social protection is to remain close to the EU, probably in a Norwegian-style relationship that allows us to join the single market through the European Economic Area (EEA). Unfortunately we would no longer have a voice in how EU rules are made, but we could rejoin the EU at a later date if opinion changes.

The EEA option would have to be based on continuation of freedom of movement to and from Europe – the best achievement of the EU, without which capital can truly keep us imprisoned while it travels the world picking and choosing between labour forces. Granted, EU freedom of movement coexists with a brutal anti-immigrant policy at its borders. This must be fought. But achieving wider freedom of movement will not be helped by the collapse of the EU, which would kill freedom of movement for a generation. This should worry anyone who believes your place of birth should not determine what sort of life you are able to enjoy.

However, there is a huge problem with this 'damage limitation' option, in that it will replay the EU referendum debate – with those arguing for this option on the side of much of the business community, and undoubtedly being accused of trying to undermine the referendum. UKIP will have a field day if they can hold their party together.

But there is really no other option. A harder Brexit would be disastrous, politically as well as economically. The most important element will be for the centre-left parties, unions, NGOs and others to unite and ensure their voice is heard above the sound of the establishment, making a clear, progressive case for free movement.

BEYOND NEOLIBERALISM

Of course, damage limitation won't solve the long-term lack of alternatives that drove so many people to vote Brexit. The failure of social democracy to confront the politics of neoliberalism is at the heart of the problem. So a radical economic programme that goes beyond neoliberalism must be developed, and it must be international. Outside Spain, the European left has not undertaken this work since the 1980s.

We must build an alternative path to free trade on the one hand or economic nationalism on the other, one that stresses trade is a *tool* of wider social objectives and not an end in itself. So as a first step, all trade deals should be subject to environmental, human rights and workers' rights commitments – and this must be enforceable. Standards in trading countries must demonstrably increase over the lifetime of the deal. The whole goal of trade deals should be a genuine form of equal development and fair distribution of wealth produced.

Fairtrade has proved that products made in better conditions can find a market via decent labelling. Transparency is a minimum then. But we could go further and make trade easier for those that produce in decent conditions, or even better produce in cooperatives and collectives. Trade must never compromise the food security of nations, for instance by incentivising the growth of export crops over food necessary for local sustenance.

Special corporate courts obviously need to be scrapped, and replaced with mechanisms that allow citizens or communities whose rights are impinged by foreign corporations to achieve restitution – at an international level where individual governments won't cooperate. This would be easier to achieve once an international treaty to control transnational corporations is agreed, something currently being pushed by Ecuador at the UN – and consistently opposed by the UK.

Even the best form of trade doesn't make up for a good industrial strategy or the development of more democratic public services. So forms of protection have a vital place in modern economics. The key is not to protect your own industry, agriculture or services in a way that sinks your neighbour's economy or disincentives innovation.

Of course, we also want to *reduce* the role of the market in our society and our lives. Democratic experiments in new forms of public control show what this might look like. Energy democracy calls for energy provision to be removed from the hands of big corporations and placed in new, local, democratically-controlled utilities, which themselves buy from and sell to state-supported cooperatives. Jeremy Corbyn has endorsed such an approach. Similarly food sovereignty is a movement for better support for small farmers, especially those that grow organically and for local markets, to challenge the power of global food corporations.

So the trade system we envisage does not have to follow 'market knows best' diktats. It should be about international *cooperation*. Technology and skills transfer should be a primary goal of trade, fostering collaborative science and invention, rather than monopolising such things through intellectual property laws.

Such trade systems do exist, though they are nowhere near sufficiently developed. The 'pink tide' governments in Latin America developed an alternative trade system known as ALBA, specifically based on principles of solidarity, redistribution of wealth, and cooperation. Venezuela's oil-for-doctors programme is one small example, and even Livingstone's London got in on the act with cheaper fuel to power public transport. The potential for an international solidarity economy is huge, and well-crafted trade rules can help bring this about. In so doing, we also fight xenophobia and insularity.

TOWARDS AN INTERNATIONALIST LEFT

There is significant work to do to develop these models, and just as much work in building alliances which can convey this to an increasingly insular public. When people's experience of globalisation is simply unemployment, commodification and marginalisation, it's easy to jump on a nationalist agenda, especially when it depicts itself as anti-establishment.

Tactically, there are opportunities. Democracy is the simplest route to bring these issues to mass attention. The British parliament has less power to scrutinise trade deals than the European parliament, and it's perfectly possible for such deals to sail through Westminster with no scrutiny at all, let alone a vote. The current government's post-Brexit power grab is beginning to alarm even its own backbenchers – which means this is a perfect time to campaign for the opening up of public and parliamentary scrutiny of trade deals, and international relations more generally.

Despite one of the biggest victories on trade for many years, with TTIP, the left has, post Brexit, lost most of its ground on the economic debate. Our task is to develop economic models which are open, international, collaborative *and* local and democratic. The left urgently needs to develop a clear and compelling vision for international economics that taps into the concerns of those who voted for Brexit, while preserving the internationalist outlook of those on the left who wanted to remain. Such models are the only hope we have of preventing a further decline into nationalism, based on a fear of the foreigner.

Nick Dearden is Director of Global Justice Now.

Norway, Switzerland or Albania? Whose relations with the EU?

TOM O'LEARY

The Brexit referendum campaign was dominated by assertions that the UK economy could benefit from access to or participation in the EU Single Market while opting out of the conditions on freedom of movement for workers. These assertions are false. This was continued during the strange Tory leadership contest, which had more casualties than debates, and has been repeated by the new Prime Minister and some of her key allies. This is a reactionary myth, with the potential to do great harm to the economy.

The former Justice Secretary and chair of the official Leave campaign Michael Gove dropped a bombshell in the Brexit campaign that not only would the UK be leaving the EU, which was on the ballot, but that a Leave vote meant we would be departing the Single Market too, which was not on the ballot. Gove made this highly damaging pledge because he followed the logic of the two official campaigns, which had been fought primarily on the terrain of anti-immigration. He understood that there was no realistic possibility of restricting freedom of movement for workers while remaining inside the Single Market.

Like Farage, Gove was effectively choosing impoverishment and lower immigration over prosperity and higher immigration.

It was largely dismissed with derision, as Gove said the model would not be Norway's or Switzerland's relations with the EU, but those of Albania. All three countries are outside the EU. But Switzerland and Norway are part of the Single Market whereas Albania is not. Switzerland and Norway both have to accept all the conditions of access to the Single Market including freedom of movement (and pay far higher per capita contributions to the EU Budget than the UK does).

Elsewhere, confusion on the relationship between the Single Market and freedom of movement continues to dominate public discussion on this topic post-referendum. It is also in danger of infecting the debate inside the labour movement. For both reasons, it is necessary to set out the correct position:

– Under current circumstances and for the foreseeable future membership of the EU Single Market is crucial to the prosperity of the UK economy; living standards will fall outside it
– The freedom of movement is a fundamental pillar of the Single Market, not an add-on or trade-off with it
– In both cases, the Single Market and its freedom of movement component raise living standards in this country greater than they would otherwise be
– The notion that it is possible to negotiate with the EU to access the Single Market while restricting freedom of movement is false. It is unacceptable to the EU as a whole.

THE NATURE OF A MARKET

A market allows the exchange of commodities. Any capitalist economy is a market on a grander scale, a series of interlocking markets. This exchange allows for what Adam Smith called the division of labour. Marx's more precise term was the socialisation of production. This is the most powerful force in economic development. Adam Smith's *Wealth of Nations* was devoted to the outworkings of the division of labour. For Marx, the socialisation of production is the economic base of socialism.

To illustrate this point, no-one reading this piece on a

laptop or a phone built that laptop or phone themselves. In a modern economy even the technology we have come to take for granted relies on a vast array of inputs of basic goods, different stages in the production process and an army of hundreds of thousands of workers to produce those goods, to develop, refine, market, transport, sell and service them and their various components. This army and this production process take place across continents. Adam Smith argued it would take an enormous time for a single labourer to create just one pin from scratch. It would take an eternity to create a laptop from one individual's labour.

Of course, the exchange of commodities in the market is unequal. The owners of the means of production can claim for themselves a huge proportion of the value created by the labour of others (which is one of the arguments for the common ownership of the means of production). But the benefits of the division of labour/socialisation of production cannot take place at all without the exchange that a market allows.

So too is the exchange between countries unequal. Many economies, most of them former colonies, were unable to develop domestic industry before the whole world was already dominated by huge multinational enterprises. They often need to restrict access to their markets in order to develop domestic industry. This is a trade-off as costs are higher and technology necessarily poorer. But it is entirely legitimate for an oppressed country to take this detour so that it can later enter the world market. Britain is not an oppressed country.

In both cases, the optimal rate of development is ultimately produced by fully participating in the division of labour/socialisation of production. But because markets allocate resources on the basis of profit, not human needs, the optimal rate of development of the economy is when the market is allowed to fly freely within the iron cage of the state.

CONTINENTAL-SIZED ECONOMIES

The superiority of the capitalist system over its predecessors lay largely in its ability to harness the productive capacity of the whole economy and raise it up to a higher level. This was initiated on the basis of the nation-state, which necessitated in most countries sweeping away feudal domains, princes and kings, as well as their laws and restrictions on all the factors of production to create a single market. Those factors of production are goods, capital and labour. But as soon as feudalism was overthrown and supplanted by capitalism, most classically in the case of the Britain, production began to penetrate overseas markets. Capitalism necessarily created modern nations and immediately began to operate internationally.

In the modern era, entire economies are being organised on a continental basis and integrating into the world economy through that medium. The growth rate of trade within those continents is growing far faster than their external trade. North America, China and the EU are continental-sized economies. India may soon join them and it is to be hoped that so too will Latin America and Africa.

Irrespective of its size, to develop the potential of any market there must be free movement, distribution and exchange of commodities within that market. One of those commodities is labour. It would be impossible to imagine, say, a properly functioning market to build houses where bricks, wood, slates and so on could be freely exchanged, and builders were free to borrow to pay for them, but labour was excluded. The whole economy includes all sectors and construction serves here as just one illustrative sector. Freedom of movement of labour is integral to the optimal function of any market.

THE EU SINGLE MARKET

It is widely understood that the EU Single Market is vital to the maintenance of living standards in the UK. Even most of the Leave campaign leaders still want access to the Single Market.

The greatest vulnerability in the current crisis is unlikely to be trade, even though new tariffs are likely to raise prices and cut exports to a certain degree. The bigger negative response is likely to be felt in terms of investment.

All large-scale firms operating internationally, wherever they are located, achieve market position and dominance by directing their activities towards the largest possible market; the UK's vote to retreat from the EU will deter some proportion of large-scale investment, either by firms based in Britain or firms which might otherwise have invested here. Unless there were radically different economic policies where the state directs the bulk of investment, which is not on offer in a country like Britain, then any economy dependent mainly on private investment will suffer outside the Single Market.

The EU and all its major component economies and political parties are committed to the operation of the Single Market including the freedom of movement. However they rationalise this, it derives from an understanding that they too would suffer economically if the Single Market were broken up. They are committed to freedom of movement as an integral part of the Single Market for the same reason. Quite literally, it is only Little Englandism which opposes free movement.

Therefore the notion that effective membership of the Single Market can be achieved while restricting free movement of workers is a fantasy. It is a reactionary fantasy because it implies that freedom of movement is a negative factor, unlike the movement of goods, capital and firms. Michael Gove recognised the unreality of being in the Single Market and promising to cut immigration, and so opted for the Albanian model. The EU cannot adopt that model, or allow others to while accessing the Single Market. Every train, lorry, car and van crossing borders would need to be opened to check whether the driver and passengers had the right to reside in the country.

Now that the Tory party has done its blood-letting, at least for now, its Brexit negotiations will be obliged to return to the real world. It is imperative that the Labour Party stands for policies that will raise the living standards of the population. In that context, this means committing to membership of the Single Market and of course the free movement of workers that makes it possible.

Tom O'Leary is an economist who writes for *Socialist Economic Bulletin.*

Brexit, racism, and the crisis of European capitalism

NEIL FAULKNER

The EU referendum campaign and the Brexit victory have thrown the small, fragmented, squabbling British left into crisis. We are witness to a failure of analysis on an historic scale, and a collapse into near-total irrelevance.

Let us be clear. The EU is a bankers' club under oligarchic control, hard-wired for austerity and privatisation. It is a vast mechanism for hoovering wealth from the working people of Europe to the 1%. It is powered by the grotesque greed of the rich and the system of parasitic capital accumulation over which they preside.

This, however, is irrelevant to Brexit. The referendum was not a choice between the EU and socialism; it was a choice between the EU and the British state – a choice that is, between a capitalist racket run from Brussels and a capitalist racket run from the City of London.

A 'LEXIT' ARGUMENT FOR VOTING LEAVE?

Socialists who argued – and in some cases continue to argue – that the Brexit vote was a 'class vote' are seriously, and dangerously, deluded. The argument goes something like this.

> *Leave voters were disproportionately poor and working class, and disproportionately concentrated in socially distressed areas. Deep-rooted discontent has expressed itself in a vote against the political and corporate elite and their European mega-project. The Brexit vote represents a vote against austerity and privatisation. It constitutes a left-wing victory and heralds an upsurge in class struggle.*

This is wrong at every point. Let us examine the argument in detail.

1. *Leave voters were disproportionately poor and working class, and disproportionately concentrated in socially distressed areas.*

The referendum statistics are these. Voting Remain were: 80% of Green voters; 75% of young people; 75% of black people; 70% of Muslims; 65% of Labour voters; and 65% of SNP voters.

I cannot find figures for this, but my guess is that between two-thirds and three-quarters of trade unionists will also have voted Remain. This is based on three things: a) ten top union leaders called for this; b) Labour's Remain vote implies it; and c) union membership is much higher among skilled public-sector workers than among unskilled private-sector workers, and the figures show 60% in the corresponding ABC1 categories voting Remain, as against 35% in the C2DE categories. (For those who are not aware, trade union membership is approximately 50% in the public sector, but only about 15% in the private sector.)

Then we have the more anecdotal evidence from further afield, like the Homerton Hospital surgical team who, protesting against Brexit, posted an online photo of themselves with national labels, showing a British (Pakistani) consultant alongside an Irish radiographer, a German consultant anaesthetist, a Greek urologist, and three Spanish scrub nurses.

What sort of socialist strategy is it that orients on the more backward, unorganised sections of the working class? What sort of strategy for radical change does not foreground the young, the unionised workers, and the Labour voters?

The stupidity is breathtaking. It is to make a nonsense of any distinction between 'class in itself' and 'class for itself': a vital distinction for Marx, who knew the great difference there was between the mere fact of class position – a matter of socio-logical description – and conscious mass struggle by working people acting for themselves to change the world. Indeed, in some sense, the whole of socialist activity is accounted for by this distinction.

2. *Deep-rooted discontent has expressed itself in a vote against the political and corporate elite and their European mega-project.*

That there are great pools of bitterness and alienation at the base of society is obvious. The question is: who gives leadership to the discontent and turns it into a political force? We are now eight years into a second great depression. It may be shallower and slower than that of the 1930s – so far – but it shows every sign of being more intractable. It is the crisis of a highly dysfunctional form of international capitalism which emerged in the 1970s and 1980s. Let us give it a name: global financialised monopoly-capitalism – a phase in the development of the system characterised by permanent stagnation-slump rooted in chronic over-accumulation of capital.

In a crisis, the centre cannot hold. There is polarisation to the left and the right. The discontent can be organised by what Trotsky called 'the party of revolutionary hope' (the socialists) or 'the party of counter-revolutionary despair' (the fascists). Central to his argument was the fact that these polar opposites drew upon the same pools of discontent in a context of global capitalist crisis.

The EU referendum was not a right/left contest. It was not an argument between capitalism and socialism, between the 1% and the working class. It was essentially a Tory split that pitted a hard right against a soft right. Of critical importance is the fact that the Lexit voice – the socialist argument for Leave – was totally inaudible in mainstream politics. The vast majority of voters made their decision on the basis of arguments presented by rival groups of neoliberal politicians – for the simple reason that they heard no others.

The Brexiters employed two main arguments. The first was an anti-state argument. 'We need to take back control' was the refrain. This control, we were told, was in the hands of EU bureaucrats. Popular hatred of the political and corporate elite was thus channelled against one section of it (the Euro elite) by another section of it (the Tory right).

The second argument was anti-immigrant. In this case, popular discontent arising from the growing poverty at the base of society was directed against other sections of the working class. The explicit argument was that immigrants from the EU were the problem. The implicit argument – as always in racist discourse – was that anybody 'not like us' was the problem. Thus, the blowback from Brexit is affecting British Muslims every bit as much as Polish migrant workers.

Both arguments are, of course, paralleled by those of the interwar fascists. The Brexit campaign was an anti-EU, anti-Westminster, anti-Establishment campaign – just as Hitler's campaign was anti-Weimar in 1932. The Brexit campaign drew upon great pools of bitterness among those at the bottom of society, the victims of globalisation, neoliberalism, and austerity – just as Hitler was supported by the unemployed, the unorganised workers, the broken small businesses, the 'little people' who felt forgotten, ignored, and abused. And the Brexit campaign fanned a great upsurge of anti-immigrant racism – just as Hitler's thugs attacked the Jews.

3. *The Brexit vote represents a vote against austerity and privatisation. It constitutes a left-wing victory and heralds an
upsurge in class struggle.*

The economic class struggle has been at rock-bottom for
about 25 years. Nothing has come close in significance to either
the miners' strike of 1984/5 or the poll tax revolt of 1989/90 in
the period since. We have seen great political upsurges, most notably against imperialism and war, but union power in the work-
places has been hollowed out by the neoliberal counter-revolution, and the strike rate has now been bumping along the bottom,
at mid-nineteenth century levels, for a quarter of a century.

We are failing to defend the most basic gains of the postwar boom. Welfare is being cut and cut and cut. The NHS is being privatised. Graduates enter working life with massive debts
because higher education has become a commodity, not a right.
There is an unprecedented housing crisis because council es-
tates have been sold off, new social housing has not been built,
and rent controls disappeared long ago in a Thatcherite 'bon-
fire of regulations'.

The working class is not on the brink of a great offensive.
It is not even holding the line in a successful defensive. It is, in
fact, retreating in disorder.

Again, comparison with Weimar Germany is not misplaced.
The example is more extreme, but that enables us to see underlying tendencies more clearly. The German Communists welcomed
the terminal crisis of Weimar Germany in 1932 with the notion
'after Hitler, our turn'. They failed to identify the main threat and
the urgent need for a defensive battle by a united working class.
The crisis is not yet of this kind, but the mistake of dogmatic Lexiters is identical: an inability to understand that the rise of the far
right across Europe is a clear and present danger, and that Brexit
Britain is a project driven by the right, not the left.

Let us, for a moment, pursue the comparison in a different
way. I have said that the crisis this time is shallower and slower,

but more intractable. I think that has major implications for its political expression. In Berlin in 1932, Vienna in 1934, and Barcelona in 1936, the struggle took the form of open clashes between armed militias. But the economic downturn, the social collapse, and the consequent political polarisation had been more rapid and extreme. Equally important, the left, rooted in a strong working-class movement with high levels of industrial militancy and street action, had to be physically confronted and smashed if the fascists were to break through. Hitler and Franco faced great working-class movements created during the revolutionary upsurge of 1917-23. By contrast, contemporary proto-fascist politicians like Donald Trump, Nigel Farage, Marine Le Pen, Viktor Orban, Milos Zeman, and others face a labour movement hollowed out by 30 years of defeat and retreat. I was one of those who used to sneer at the notion of 'creeping fascism'. Not any more; the far right does not need an army of Brownshirts to make headway in early twenty-first century Europe (or America).

AN AGE OF UNREASON

In the eighteenth century, when the new capitalist system was emerging from the cocoon of the *ancien regime*, it spawned an 'Age of Reason' – an age of free enquiry, scientific experiment, new inventions, radical ideas, and all-out assault on ignorance, superstition, and bigotry. But this 'Enlightenment' – a giant leap in human civilisation fostered by the rising bourgeoisie – was short-lived. Because capitalism offered freedom to the few at the expense of the many – because the new rich were greatly outnumbered by the new proletariat – the human intellect had to be returned to the darkness. The main ideological props of the new capitalist world order became nationalism and racism. Since the time of the British Chartists and the Paris Commune – since, that is, the spectre of socialist revolution first cast its shadow across the counting-houses of capital – humanity has been presented with two main alternatives: nationalism, racism, imperialism, and war on one side; socialism, democracy, and peace on the other.

All political action must, in the final analysis, be judged according to whether it advances the cause of international working-class revolution or impedes it. Capitalism is inherently exploitative, violent, and oppressive. It is incapable of serving the needs of humanity. It constitutes a mortal threat to both human and environmental well-being. Given that, the system must be overthrown and replaced with another based on equality, democracy, and sustainability. And the only conceivable mechanism for such change is collective mass action by working people.

That is why working-class unity in struggle is the very essence of socialist praxis. Achieving this means overcoming everything that divides and therefore weakens us. It means relentless exposure and criticism of what Marx called 'the crap of ages' – the sexism and racism, the nationalism and flag-waving, the snobbery and sneering, the awful business of 'tuppence-ha'penny' looking down on 'tuppence', and all the other stuff whose effect is to divide and disable our side.

This is the only real context for making judgements about Brexit. We have to ask: what does it mean in terms of working-class consciousness? Will it make it easier for workers to unite and fight? Or will it drive wedges into the class? Will it leave working people following the lead of nationalists and neoliberals, and, in their despair and bewilderment, turning on other working people?

The ideological dichotomy that preoccupies me here – the age-long contest between nation and class – is central to the Brexit debate. Because what we are seeing on the right is the eruption of an increasingly virulent form of racially-charged nationalism that we fail to recognise at our peril.

So as to understand it better, I want to situate this political expression of the crisis in its economic context.

PERMANENT STAGNATION-SLUMP

The European economy is mired in a long-term crisis of stagnation-slump. This crisis has its roots in the 1970s, when the 'state-capitalist' model of economic development broke down, having been destabilised and eventually brought to ruin by the rise of the transnational mega-corporation.

The real meaning of 'globalisation' is that the territory of the nation-state ceases to be the main locus of capital accumulation, and that the state loses its role as a manager of accumulation and is reduced to its traditional role as servant of capital – only now, not the national capital of home-based firms, but the internationalised capital of global conglomerates. Instead, then, of a proactive state exercising a wide measure of economic control, direction, and regulation – so as to overcome monopoly capital's inherent tendency towards what Keynes called 'permanent underemployment equilibrium' – we have states engaged in a bidding war to attract private investment by cutting taxes, selling public services, breaking unions, and driving down wages.

This does not mean 'the end of the state'. The state remains essential to the functioning of capitalism. It provides vital infrastructure. It succours the labour force. It turns tax revenues into sources of corporate profit by issuing state contracts and selling off public property. It polices social discontent and crushes organised resistance. It projects military power overseas to further corporate interests. But it does not run nationalised industries, direct industrial investment, control capital flows, or regulate exchange rates. And the fact that it no longer does so reflects a qualitative shift from a 'state-capitalist' stage of development to a 'neoliberal' one in which the dominant firms – the great corporate 'movers and shakers' of the world economy – have become true 'transnationals', their global reach putting them beyond effective control by nation-states. Capital, in short, has burst the national shell.

The result is permanent stagnation-slump. The reason is

this. The giant corporations which dominate each global market operate as informal cartels to create demand, manage sales, and sustain prices. They are therefore in a position to avoid mutually damaging forms of price competition, being few enough to collaborate to prevent this; they become 'price-makers' rather than 'price-takers'. Reduced competition in managed markets means reduced pressure to invest in new production facilities in order to keep abreast of rival firms. A further disincentive to investment is the sheer mass of capital required to create new world-standard facilities: a big modern plant is often just too expensive and too long-term in an uncertain world. So the corporations become risk-averse, investment falls, and growth slows.

This creates a 'scissors crisis' for the system. Monopoly means higher consumer prices and more corporate profit; that is, a rising proportion of the social surplus going to capital as opposed to labour. But monopoly also means reduced competition and therefore lower investment. So the mass of profit/surplus rises, but relative demand – both from workers for consumption and capitalists for investment – falls. The system ends up awash with surplus capital unable to find an outlet in productive investment. Stagnation-slump becomes the norm.

The 'neoliberal counter-revolution' was an attempt to solve the crisis of the 1970s by launching a frontal attack on unions, wages, and the welfare state. The aim was to redistribute wealth from labour to capital. Higher profit, argued Thatcher and Reagan, would encourage enterprise, investment, and growth.

In fact, it merely intensified the scissors crisis of 'over-accumulation' (of capital) and 'under-consumption' (by workers). The dead weight of surplus capital being carried by the global economy steadily increased. Cuts in wages and public spending drained demand. The resulting contradiction – in Keynesian terms, a failure of 'aggregate demand' – gave rise to financialisation. Instead of investing in production, the corporations – both financial and industrial – invested their surplus capital in the money markets. They began trading on a massive scale in debt – state debt, corporate debt, and consumer debt.

The statistics are eye-watering. By the end of the last century, 95% of all currency trading was speculative – that is, it was not to facilitate the exchange of real goods, but to make money on changing relative values. Immediately before the 2008 crash, the trade in derivatives – debt-based financial assets – was estimated to have had a value of $500 trillion, equal to ten times global GDP. The value of debt and speculation in Britain was running at round five times the value of the real economy. Across the EU, bank assets were worth about 350% of total European GDP. Debt grew from 1.5 times US national output in the early 1980s to nearly 3.5 in 2007. The financial sector's share of US profits had increased from about 15% in the early 1950s to almost 50% in 2001.

This system – global financialised monopoly-capitalism – is parasitic and pathological. The real economy is in permanent stagnation-slump. The bubble economy of hyper-charged trade in debt – typically anchored in real estate – is now the dominant form of capital accumulation. Nothing is actually being produced. No new value is being created. The rich are simply gobbling up wealth by gambling in financial assets. What is the ultimate source of this wealth? It is working people, who are being exploited as workers, consumers, and debtors: they are the foundation block of real wealth on which rests the financial edifice of casinos, speculation, and greed.

So the neoliberal counter-revolution has failed. It smashed organised labour, raised the rate of profit, and opened up a range of alternative mechanisms for continued capital accumulation. Financialisation – essentially profiting from debt and the exploitation of workers at the point of consumption as opposed to the point of production – is the most important such mechanism. Privatisation – essentially the sale of public services to create new revenue streams for private capital – is another. What neoliberalism was unable to do however, was address the underlying problem of lack of productive investment in the real economy in a global system dominated by transnational corporate giants. It was the growing contradiction between financial speculation and actual production, of course, which produced the 2008 crash.

We have now, in consequence, entered a new global depression. It differs from the last in that there appears to be no 'bourgeois' solution: no equivalent of the Keynesian 'state-capitalist' fix of the 1940s. Instead, unable to imagine any alternative, the international ruling class continues to chant the neoliberal mantras of the 1990s. The banks remain casinos for the super-rich. The conglomerates continue to buy up public services. The rich get richer, the living standards of workers stagnate, the poor are screwed, and the NHS is sold off to profiteers. Historic levels of alienation from the political and corporate elite are inevitable: the system is broken, society is being torn apart, and our rulers are corrupt and self-serving. And because of all this, politics is rotten with nationalism, racism, and pent-up rage.

Some socialists have argued that the EU is the European elite's mega-project, that Brexit has thrown this project into crisis, and that this represents an opportunity for the left. They argue that Brexit is a disaster for the Tories – that the government has been divided and destabilised by the outcome of the EU referendum. The argument appears to be a desperate attempt to avoid admitting a serious mistake. The simple fact is that a new government has been formed and that May is fully in control and well ahead in the polls. It is the Labour Party, of course, that is in crisis; and it has continued in crisis even after the second leadership election, because the main fracture line in British politics – between neoliberalism and some sort of anti-austerity alternative – runs through the middle of it, pitting right-wing career politicians against socialist activists representing the interests of working people.

THE SECURITY STATE

The state is in retreat from two key roles: that of economic management, and that of welfare provision. This retreat reflects the domination of the global economy by transnational corporate giants. The state-capitalist/Keynesian period imposed one set of functions on the state. The epoch of global financialised monopoly-capitalism imposes another. The state becomes more repressive. Unable to manage economic life or make social provision in the interests of the people – unable, that is, to curtail the ravages of a world driven by capital accumulation and corporate profit – it becomes instead a security apparatus for controlling an alienated, discontented, sullen working class.

Society is increasingly atomised by the weakening of union power and the retreat of the welfare state. Collective organisation, social solidarity, and public provision are being dissolved. Society is becoming fragmented and atomised. Individuals are finding themselves exposed and vulnerable – bullied as workers, ripped off as consumers, disenfranchised as citizens.

So we inhabit a world of stagnation-slump, of corporate power, and of debt; a world of parasitic greed at the top, and of poverty, stress, and despair at the bottom; a world in which public service decays and security police multiply; a world of alienation and fear. And the right seeks to harness that alienation and fear, and, in the context of the War on Terror and Brexit, to direct it against Muslims and migrants, 'terrorists' and 'scroungers' – against, that is, some sort of alien 'other' against which we must defend ourselves.

Make no mistake: this dystopian neoliberal social order, and the poisonous ideology it has spawned, is the seedbed of twenty-first century fascism. In the absence of a strong left – which means a left based on powerful working-class organisation and a compelling vision of the world transformed – the political monsters now emerging from the social depths may engulf us.

We need an alternative and we need a movement. Perhaps

the surge of enthusiasm and activity around Jeremy Corbyn's leadership of the Labour Party is the embryo of these. It is good to see that some serious policies are finally being advanced – for a national bank, for a public-investment programme, for the reversal of NHS privatisation, and more. But if such a programme could be smashed by the opposition of international finance capital in the 1970s – which it was – how likely is it that such a programme could be implemented in 2020? What lessons, in this respect, are to be drawn from the fate of the Syriza government in Greece in 2015? Is it not the case – given the centralisation and concentration of capital today, given the even greater domination of the global economy by corporate giants, given the unprecedented accumulations of wealth and power at the top of the international social order – that the only hope for working people is united mass struggle on the widest possible international scale?

Yet whole sections of the British left are in denial about the wave of nationalism and racism unleashed by the Brexit vote – about the shift to the right that it represents. We need to recognise the danger, unite around the demand for free movement, and work with our European comrades to build resistance to the rule of bankers, bosses, and bureaucrats across the continent.

Neil Faulkner is the author of *A Marxist History of the World: from Neanderthals to Neoliberals.*